I Wish
I Knew
This
Earlier

I Wish I Knew This Earlier

Lessons on Love

Toni Tone

4th ESTATE · London

4th Estate
An imprint of HarperCollins*Publishers*
1 London Bridge Street
London SE1 9GF

www.4thEstate.co.uk

HarperCollins*Publishers*
Macken House, 39/40 Mayor Street Upper,
Dublin1, D01 C9W8, Ireland

First published in Great Britain in 2021 by 4th Estate

5

Copyright © Toni Tone 2021

A catalogue record for this book is
available from the British Library

ISBN 978-0-00-845824-9

Set in Adobe Garamond Pro
Printed and bound in the UK using 100%
renewable electricity at CPI Group (UK) Ltd

MIX
Paper | Supporting
responsible forestry
FSC™ C007454

This book is produced from independently certified FSC™ paper
to ensure responsible forest management.

For more information visit: www.harpercollins.co.uk/green

Contents

Foreword

One question I'm asked a lot is what advice would I give to my younger self? In truth, I'd tell my younger self to just keep going, because everything I've done has led me to this moment. It has led me to writing this book for you. But let's pretend for a moment that I would still have written this book regardless of the choices I made when I was younger. In that case, I would most certainly give myself advice about love; this book is a manifestation of that. Why love? Love ties all of us together. Despite what some people might say, I believe we all crave it, we all want it, and we all love how love can make us feel. I love talking about love and reading about love, so it only makes sense for me to write about it too.

This book contains the lessons that would have been very useful to the younger me – lessons I wish I knew earlier. I want to be the big sister I didn't get access to. I want to introduce lessons from my past, which might help to shape your future for the better. These lessons were picked up in various ways: some through observing others, some through reading, some through listening, some through feeling and many through making my own mistakes.

In this book I want to share these learnings with you, in the hope that it may change your life. I'm sure many of the lessons I've included are things you've read or heard before, but I know how easy it is to forget the valuable nuggets and gems we pick up throughout life. Sometimes we just need to be reminded of things we already know. Sometimes we need to bring those things to the forefront of our mind and alight our subconscious. Sometimes we need a nudge and that's how we change our life. My hope is that you finish this book feeling like you will navigate relationships in a healthier, wiser and happier way.

This book is made up of three key sections: the dating stage, the loving stage and the healing stage. The dating stage' covers the lessons I learned about getting to know people romantically. 'The loving stage' explores being in love with someone and the lessons I picked up about developing a healthy and happy relationship. 'The healing stage' touches on the painful topic of heartbreak and breakups.

One thing I want you to know is that you can read this book in the order that feels most relevant to your story and journey right now. Some of you will be experiencing post-breakup blues, so it only makes sense for you to want to jump straight into 'the healing stage'. Do it. Read the section that you want to read right now, and the others can follow. Similarly, if you're in a relationship and want to know more about what I learned from my own, feel free to start with 'the loving stage', and if you think you've just met the potential love of your life, get stuck into 'the dating stage'. I want my book to work for you, so read it in the order that makes the most sense to you.

Lastly, I want to stress something before you begin reading some of these lessons. I often hear people say, 'life is a journey, not a race', and it's true. Life is not something people just 'figure out'. We are constantly growing, learning, adapting and changing, and because of that we can never have all the answers at once. I for one don't have all the answers and I'm on this journey called life with you. The lessons in this book reflect the person I am today and the experiences I have had to date. You may read certain lessons and love them. You may read other lessons and disagree with them. I expect that. I want this book to generate open and honest conversations. So if you love something you read, talk about it. If you don't like something you read, talk about it. As I type this now, I'm open to learning more with you, so being the digitally savvy writer that I am, talk to me – *#IWIKTE*.

Section 1:
The Dating Stage

Dating isn't something that is taught to us formally and many of us have 'learned' how to date from watching television, speaking to friends or simply just figuring it out as we go along. For the majority of people, the latter is most true. This is my story. I had no big sister or brother at home to talk me through the complexities of getting to know people on a romantic level, so as the oldest child, I had to figure things out by myself.

I started dating at sixteen, and, like me, many people first jump into the dating scene as teenagers and their experience during this time is largely based on trial and error. This trial and error period comes with making many mistakes – some of which we carry on into adulthood. Many of these mistakes are shaped by society and how the world views the roles of women and men, coupled with how we view ourselves.

In this section of my book, I'm going to share several lessons I picked up through making my own mistakes, doing things right and watching people navigate their own dating lives. My hope is that after reading these lessons, you will reflect on your own dating life and you will consider some of the things you do well, do badly and should probably change. I want this section of the book to help you make better decisions for yourself. I made a few wrong decisions growing up, and many of these lessons are lessons I wish I knew earlier.

Date people who want the same things as you

Dating is easier to navigate when we know what we want to get out of the process. When we have a better understanding of what we're looking for, we have a better understanding of what we will and won't accept. We also do a better job of communicating our needs and wants to people.

One mistake I made in the past was dating people without really understanding what I genuinely wanted. At times I would find myself in relationships with people not because I truly wanted to be with them, but because everything around me suggested I should have a relationship. I would end up with people not because they possessed the characteristics I deeply desired in a partner, but because they were persistent, and I was single. Suddenly I'd be in a relationship and I'd find myself thinking, 'is this what you *really* want?'. Another mistake I made was knowing what I wanted, but dating people who wanted a completely different type of relationship to me. I went along with their vision, and I only realised their vision wouldn't work with mine when it was too late.

We can sometimes underestimate the value of having some direction before dating. Having direction doesn't mean we know exactly where we will end up at all times. Having direction is about knowing where we *want* to go, which often leads to us taking helpful steps towards getting there. This doesn't mean you have to enter the dating world with a very serious plan mapped out. Just consider what is driving you. Prior to dating a person, it's helpful to have a good understanding of what exactly it is you're trying to get out of it. Do you want something casual? Are you looking for a monogamous relationship? Would you prefer an open relationship? Do you want to date someone who is ready to find a life partner? Do you want to get married and have children? Knowing what you want will help to guide your dating style, and accepting what you want will also help you to communicate your wants to romantic interests.

What happens when people don't know what they want? They may find themselves stuck in unproductive relationships. They may veer away from committing to anything because they are uncertain about their desires. They may become more easily distracted because they're in a relationship which doesn't truly meet their wants. They may be too reliant on others for guidance because they don't know what they want to achieve. They may resent their partner for leading them in a direction they don't want to go in. They may find themselves where they shouldn't be, because they have no idea where they want to be.

Knowing what you want to get out of dating enables you to be more honest with people and in turn, more fulfilled. When you know how you want your life to turn out, you're in a better position to make clear and concrete decisions surrounding your relationships. This leads to having more open and honest conversations with prospective partners. Too often, people can find themselves unintentionally leading other people on, simply because they want different things from their partner but they haven't asserted what they want, and as a result, when it's time to take a significant step in the relationship, they retreat.

It's important that you have an idea of what you're looking for from a relationship. Perhaps you're not even looking for a relationship at all? Just have an understanding of your needs and wants. Whatever you're looking for, be clear about it with the people in your life. Allow them to make informed decisions when it comes to dating you, and if they don't want the same things as you, you're better off finding someone who does.

Our comfort zones are not always healthy

> *Just because a person or situation feels familiar and you feel comfortable, doesn't necessarily mean it's right for you. Chaos and emotional unavailability can feel familiar to a person who grew up around both. People can feel comfortable in high stress environments. If absence of peace is all someone has ever known, peace can generate discomfort.*

When I was 31, I had a very open and candid conversation with my dad about my childhood, and the ways I felt he could have been a better father. Don't get me wrong – my dad is a wonderful dad in many ways, but, like most parents, he didn't always get things right. Our discussion included a range of things, but for the purpose of this love lesson, one thing we discussed was his inability to control his emotions at times, and the things he said in anger. Following our emotional heart-to-heart, he wrote me a letter, apologising for past behaviours, and shared how proud he was of me. My dad is a very loving man in many ways, and I'm blessed to have a father who is willing to listen to constructive criticism and apologise for his mistakes. I love him dearly, but I did have to unlearn being comfortable in certain situations that I was very used to because of some of the things I experienced as a child.

I had a childhood that was wonderful for the most part, but there were periods that involved a great deal of stress. Perhaps you can relate? Perhaps your parents had certain character flaws? Perhaps, due to this, you grew used to being around certain types of people or being in certain types of environments? Maybe so much so that what was actually negative, felt normal to you? Or maybe your parents didn't shape your negative comfort zones at all? Perhaps all your previous romantic relationships had something negative in common and that's where your comfort zone stems from? Whatever the source of the stress may have been, it's very easy for people to grow accustomed to stress when they've been exposed to heavy doses of it.

For some people, their comfort zone is chaos, so stepping out of their comfort zone actually means stepping into calm, stepping into peace and stepping into a stable and consistently loving environment.

My parents have been married for over thirty years and their relationship is the best it has ever been, but dealing with my dad's mood swings as a child meant I became very used to instability. In fact, it was the norm for me. Things might be good for a few weeks, or a few months, and then they wouldn't be so good again. I expected major fluctuations in relationships. I thought it was normal to have regular arguments. I would be sceptical when things were peaceful for too long, and that's how 'chaos' felt comfortable to me.

If you can relate to my story to some degree, I imagine the thought of a peaceful relationship was once foreign to you, or maybe it still is? Maybe you are familiar with feeling on edge, experiencing aggression, seeing a lack of trust, maybe even being in a constant state of panic?

Some people I've spoken to in life, such as friends and online acquaintances, are actually comfortable with absence and emotional unavailability. Unlike me, who had a very present parent that experienced mood swings at times; some people had a very absent parent – who was either never around or rarely around, and very emotionally unavailable. As such, they feel comfortable.

with partners who are aloof, and who come in and out of their life as they please. This familiarity means they are actually attracted to people who are somewhat flaky, hard to read and not very open with their emotions. As a result, open, transparent, loving, communicative and forthcoming people can come across 'intense' or even 'weird' to them.

It can be an overwhelming revelation when you come to the conclusion that your comfort zone isn't healthy.

At this point, I imagine you're probably wondering what I did to change my comfort zone. Well the work actually started long before I had that conversation with my dad when I was 31. Prior to that chat, we had other smaller talks, so I had known for a very long time that I had to unlearn certain things. The first step I had to take was being honest with myself in determining what I was and wasn't comfortable with. That's also what you need to do.

It's very important for all of us to ask ourselves what we are comfortable with. Ask yourself what you are drawn to. Ask yourself whether you have pushed healthy relationships away. Ask yourself if you have ever gravitated towards toxicity. One helpful way to do this is to write a list of what your exes have in common. If you don't have exes, really consider whether positive qualities in people have turned you off them. Do you find people who are willing to be vulnerable, weak? Do you think people who enjoy your company are needy? You may discover that you've grown to feel comfortable in unhealthy environments or relationships. You might find that you're so used to 'less' that you talk yourself out of attaining 'more'.

If you come to the conclusion that you are drawn to some negative personality or behavioural traits, there are several things you can do. The first is embark on the luxury of therapy – and I say luxury because it is one. Therapy isn't cheap and highly accessible, but if you have the means, it's one way you can dig a little deeper into your past and your preferences. The second thing you can do is to actively make the effort to 'step out of your comfort zone'. What does this involve? It's just like stepping out of your comfort zone with anything else. You do the opposite of what you would normally do, you say 'yes' to opportunities you would typically say 'no' to, and you speak to people you wouldn't usually speak to. This is what I did, and I did this enough times that I started to see what I was comfortable with as a major turn off. So try to speak to/court/date people who possess the positive qualities that make you feel uneasy. Push through the awkwardness, the 'ick', the feelings grounded in emotions that make you feel undeserving. But do be as transparent as you can be in the process – don't lead anyone on.

Your comfort zone may not be healthy, but you can change that.

Intimacy tells you more about a relationship than intensity

Intense feelings aren't always a good indicator of how good someone is for us. Sometimes they're triggered by infatuation, lust or even trauma. A better measure is intimacy. Are you friends first? Can you be vulnerable? Do you feel safe? Is there trust?

Sadly, many of us often mistake excitement, thrill and passion for love. We become obsessed with how we 'think' we should feel and prioritise 'butterflies' and 'fireworks' over genuine compatibility and intimacy.

For many people, some of their most 'intense' feelings in relationships occurred when they were younger and not necessarily at their wisest. They experienced several 'firsts' and these new experiences came with a flurry of fresh feelings and emotions.

This was certainly true for my first relationship. I had my first boyfriend at 16 and we dated until I was 18. I remember being full of butterflies when his name would appear on my phone. I remember us sneaking out of lessons to share kisses in empty classrooms, or him sneaking me into his house when his parents weren't at home. I remember the day his parents finally caught me in the house. His mother lost it and told me to leave. I remember it raining heavily, more than it had rained in a very long time. He followed me out of the house, against his mother's wishes, and consoled me in the middle of the street. We were being drenched, but we didn't care – because we were together. It was like something out of a noughties teenage romcom. I remember crying my eyes out when I was leaving for university in another city. I thought the world was going to end. It was all so intense and so dramatic. But it was intense largely because we were young, and it was new.

For other people, some of their most intense feelings occurred outside of their first relationship, but not because their relationship was pleasant and intimate, but because the person they were dating played tug of war with their emotions. The rollercoaster fuelled the intensity, which wasn't healthy.

I have also been here. The relationship which followed my first was intense for all the wrong reasons. It was a rollercoaster romance, and it's very easy to get addicted to the extremes of a rollercoaster. When things are good, they're great – but when things are bad, they're terrible.

The impact of being in a rollercoaster relationship often involves people expressing a myriad of emotions over a short space of time. This can easily lead to the belief that we are 'bonded' to a person. However, not all bonds are created equal. Some are caused by intense and emotional experiences with a toxic person. One moment you're being mistreated, the next you're being told you are the love of their life. One moment you experience intense aggression from your partner, the next moment your partner is highly affectionate. One moment you're being disrespected, the next moment they make you feel good about yourself. I experienced a lot of this, and it's no surprise that someone else who goes through similar things, may feel like they're feeling 'passionate' emotions, when in reality what they are experiencing is an unhealthy bond generated by extreme highs and lows.

A better measure than intensity is intimacy. Are you friends first? Can you be vulnerable? Do you feel safe? Is there trust?

With age I recognised the value of true intimacy. When I felt comfortable enough to strip everything away, safe enough to open up about emotions, and cared for enough to trust wholeheartedly … that's when I felt most loved. I realised it's not simply about experiencing 'fireworks' 24/7. It's about healthy togetherness – even when the fireworks are present.

Sometimes, what we 'think' we should feel in relationships can cloud our judgement. When this happens, people end up chasing 'feelings' instead of chasing someone with positive qualities. They value butterflies and passion instead of consistency, commitment and care. People can also wrongly associate butterflies and passion with certain negative behaviours (for example: someone controlling or jealous), so when they meet a person who is calm and rational, they tell themselves there is no 'passion', when in reality, there is no emotional turmoil.

Genuine compatibility is also more important than intensity. Do you gel well together? Do you have complementary communication styles? Do you have similar interests? Can you easily hold a conversation with them? Do you get on as friends? Do you hold similar values? It's very possible to feel intense emotions with people we're not truly compatible with. Sometimes, we may also find ourselves assuming we are compatible with people based on sexual compatibility alone. While sexual satisfaction is important in many relationships, emotional and mental satisfaction should be just as important. I have no doubt that compatibility and genuine intimacy has built stronger and happier relations than 'intensity' alone ever has.

Can healthy intimate relationships be intense? Of course they can. But they're usually not emotionally intense in an overwhelming way. If anything, they're calming, grounding and stable, and we are able to process our emotions with more rationale and ease. The intensity that people feel in healthy relationships often comes from a place of immense fulfilment and attraction – which is a result of finding someone you are truly compatible with.

Genuinely liking you looks like respecting you

It's one thing for someone to lust after you and spend time with you. It's another thing for someone to genuinely like you as a person. We can spend time in the company of people out of boredom, we can spend a night with people due to lust. Genuinely liking someone comes with genuinely respecting them. That is what truly makes the difference.

It seems like common sense to date people who have shown that they like you, but many people, at some point, have focused their energy on individuals they have to chase. Constantly 'auditioning' for them; regularly trying to prove their value because the person doesn't recognise it. I've seen plenty of friends do this, and I've also done this before. In the past, I've spent too much time trying to prove my value and not enough time determining the value someone else was bringing into my life. I've gone where I wasn't being celebrated.

Don't do what I did. Don't go where you're made to feel inadequate. Go where you are adored.

To stress, this doesn't mean you should be in a one-way relationship that involves never doing nice things for the person you like. It means doing nice things for the person you like, who also likes you back. Don't go above and beyond for people who haven't actually shown you that they genuinely like you. Not sure if the person you're dating truly likes you or not? If the energy you are applying to getting to know them isn't being reciprocated, that's often a clear sign. Another clear sign is whether or not they *respect* you.

I once saw a question online, asking people what they admired most in others, and there were lots of interesting answers, but mine was respect. I chose respect because it underpins so much of what makes a person a great person to be around. When someone has genuine respect for you, they respect your time, your body, your opinions, your boundaries, your decisions, etc. It doesn't matter how much somebody claims to like you or even love you if they can't respect you. Respectful people treat others with dignity and make others feel like they truly matter. Wanting to have sex with you isn't enough. Going on dates with you isn't enough. Do they actually respect you?

Invest time in people who show you that you are respected. They do not treat you like a chore, an inconvenience or a burden. Their actions don't make you feel insignificant or unimportant to them.

You deserve a love that celebrates you as you are – not one that implies you are not enough and you are not deserving of respect.

I know this now, but I wish I knew this earlier.

Don't betray yourself to find love

> *Self-betrayal is very real. Sometimes we do it in an attempt to find or keep love. It can look like saying 'yes' or 'no' to things when we really mean the opposite, deprioritising our needs to prioritise someone else, not speaking our mind, overextending ourselves or invalidating our own feelings in an attempt to keep someone happy.*

Are you someone who does or has done everything in your power to make or keep your partner happy? This can be a very unhealthy habit if you're overlooking your happiness in the process. Arguably, it's also not your job to make anyone happy. It's everyone's responsibility to be in charge of their own happiness. Your role is to support it and not disrupt it.

Self-betrayal is a common mistake some people make while dating or while in relationships. Many of us have a longing desire to be loved. A yearning for companionship is normal but sometimes this yearning can lead to us doing a disservice to ourselves.

I've self-betrayed before and at the time I didn't even realise I was doing it. Instead I told myself I didn't want to come across as 'difficult'. I told myself I didn't want to be a 'nag'. I told myself I just wanted to make my partner happy. My self-betrayal appeared in the form of keeping quiet about things that bothered me. Sometimes I would invalidate my own feelings because I didn't want to deal with confrontation and I didn't want to 'dampen the mood'. At times I accepted things I didn't want to accept. At times I pushed my preferences and desires to the side and pushed my partner's needs and desires to the centre, because deep down I wanted to be adored.

Do some people behave in this way because they are being emotionally or mentally abused in some way? Indeed. But I wouldn't call that self-betrayal. What makes self-betrayal very different from manipulation and emotional/mental abuse often lies in the way in which we view the world and ourselves. People who self-betray can exhibit these behaviours even when they're in loving relationships with caring people. In my case, I betrayed myself by doing things that nobody asked or expected of me. I was a victim of my own mindset, moulded by the way society views the role of women in relationships, cultural expectations and my attachment style – as shaped by my relationship with my parents and others around me.

As the oldest sibling, I've spent a fair share of my life being a bit of a people pleaser or a 'teacher's pet' of sorts. I wanted to do everything 'right', I wanted words of affirmation from others and I wanted to be viewed as 'ideal'. This trickled down into my adult relationships. I had a strong desire to be viewed as 'perfect', which played a huge role in my self-betrayal. I cared less about how I felt in a relationship and more about what my partner thought of me. As long as they thought of me in a positive way, I was happy. Even if I felt negative in the process.

One bit of advice from me is this: self-betrayal hinders your relationship more than it helps it.

When you self-betray, you chip away a little bit of yourself each time. What you are doing is reducing yourself to make or keep someone happy. When you reduce yourself in this way, you eventually become unhappy and your unhappiness manifests in the relationship. You need to treat yourself with the same care and love that you show to other people. You want people who are with you to be happy? Well you deserve to be happy too, and you cannot make them happy when you are presenting a reduced and broken version of yourself.

Be open about things that are bothering you. Sharing concerns in a relationship is healthy and normal. Ideally, you want to establish an environment where you and your partner can mutually air grievances, should either of you have any. It's impossible to fix something when nobody will express how it's broken. Express yourself and do yourself, your partner, and your relationship a massive favour.

Self-love is important for positive relationship experiences

> *At times, we need to take a step back from dating, because we know deep down that we are being driven by feelings of inadequacy. Sometimes we are looking for people to fill a void, validate us or heal a wound. If you recognise that there are things you need to work through, don't feel hopeless. Being able to self-reflect and consider the impact you have on your own dating experiences, demonstrates maturity and awareness.*

In my work throughout the years, I've mentioned self-love frequently. Particularly on social media and in interviews. Everyone has their own definition of self-love, but for me:

Self-love is being able to be compassionate with
yourself, appreciate yourself and recognise your
value in a way that encourages you to prioritise
your wellbeing and embark on experiences that
contribute to your happiness.

In my mid-twenties I started to learn more about the
importance of self-love, and as I did, I began to consider
the role it plays in our relationships with others. I
reflected back to my negative romantic experience in my
early twenties, and my reflections brought me to the
realisation that the experience was amplified by a lack of
self-love at the time. The reason I use the word 'amplified' is because I do not wish to absolve the other party
of responsibility. Ultimately, a lot of the darker times I
faced were largely a result of the other party's actions and
behaviour, and during my reflections, it was important
for me to not blame myself for the things they were in
control of. However, I did know it was also important
for me to consider my role in things.

The lack of self-love I had for myself at the time
showed up in the form of me not prioritising my wellbeing. Instead, I prioritised theirs and treated my own
wellbeing as if it was secondary. I also tolerated situa-

tions that did not contribute to my happiness. In fact, it was quite the opposite. Despite periods of utter unhappiness, I stuck around because deep down, I felt being in a relationship added to my value.

When I left the relationship, I did some self-work. This included trying to rebuild my confidence, trying to reaffirm the type of relationship I wanted and reminding myself of the value I have as an individual. I started a journey to boost my self-love, and in case you're wondering about the tangible things I started on this journey, here is a brief list below:

- I set small and achievable goals in my life, and I kept track of my wins. This helped to remind me that I am capable of achieving the things I want.
- I started celebrating my wins (small and large) to get me into the habit of celebrating myself.
- I kept the company of people who made me feel good about myself and who wanted to see me happy.
- I was mindful about the way I spoke to myself and the way I spoke about myself to other people.

- I took time out to do things I enjoy, like travelling. This reminded me that my life is to be lived and loved in a way that suits me.
- I practiced accepting compliments. Instead of sharing a rebuttal, I would simply say 'thank you'.
- I started setting clearer boundaries with people in my life, so I would be better at doing so in my next relationship.
- I started to hold people accountable for their own actions, instead of creating excuses for them or blaming myself for their behaviour.
- I started speaking more openly to people close to me about my feelings.
- I had to tell myself that I was deserving of good things, and I had to repeat this regularly, until it became a habit that turned into a belief.

I think it's important for me to stress that the above bullet points are things I started to do – not necessarily things I have mastered. To this day I am still working on all of these bullet points to a degree. I want you to know this because sometimes we can assume that there's some final destination associated with self-love, but it's much more complex than this. The journey to loving yourself is a lifelong one. As we age, as we face challenges, as we make mistakes, as our bodies change, as we live life; there will be moments where we don't love ourselves as much as we may have done the day before. There will also be things that we need to work on despite how long we have been on our self-love journey.

When I started implementing these bullet points, I did so to remind myself of my value. I wanted to feel more confident about asserting my boundaries and going for what I truly desire. I also wanted to do a better job of taking care of myself, and prioritising my wellbeing. I started doing these things to help me grow as a person and to feel more confident in myself and my capabilities, but I did not tell myself I had to master all of these things before I moved on to my next relationship. I remained single for a year and a half before dating again, but I dated with the knowledge that I was still working on loving myself – because self-love is a lifelong commitment after all.

When I say self-love is an important part of having positive relationships, it truly is. But I don't want you to think you need to be some all-knowing all-seeing self-love Jedi before you can love again. Fundamentally, you simply need to know that you are deserving of love and you deserve to be loved in a way that fulfils you, through contributing to your happiness and not jeopardising your mental, emotional or physical wellbeing. You need to know that being single is better than accepting anything less than this.

Compromising and settling are two different things

> 'Settling' in a relationship isn't about dating a guy who is five foot nine when you'd prefer he was six foot, or dating a girl with straight hair when you prefer curly. Settling is compromising your values and boundaries. It's being in a relationship that doesn't add to your happiness. It's disregarding your needs. It's dismissing your non-negotiables.

I've had lots of conversations throughout my life about 'settling' in a relationship and what that looks like. From my discussions, I've come to the conclusion that it looks like different things to different people, but for the purpose of this lesson, I want to share what it looks like to me.

We can sometimes assume not settling means not compromising, but I don't define settling like this. I don't define settling like this because 99.9 per cent of people who are in happy relationships have compromised in some way, but I wouldn't say they have settled. What do compromises look like? Compromises look like your dream partner being a millionaire or looking like a fashion model, and choosing to date someone who isn't. When we make compromises, we are opting for something that doesn't meet our most desirable preferences. When we compromise, we make an agreement on the basis that we are still benefiting significantly from the relationship.

It's a hard pill to swallow but the majority of people in relationships do not fit their partner's ideal material-istic specifications 100 per cent. Their partners just don't tell them. Sure, your partner may think you are the most wonderful person in the world but that doesn't necessar-ily mean they think you are the most physically attractive. I know this seems harsh, but it's reality. There will always be people who are more attractive in some way, and that's life. Perhaps your partner prefers green eyes and you have brown? Maybe they prefer a curvier or more athletic build? There will be things they like which you don't possess. Does this mean they 'settled' for you?

I define settling as selecting someone who is not meeting your needs.

I know what you're thinking … 'What if I have physical needs that aren't being met because I'm not attracted to my partner?'. Attraction is certainly important, and I believe you need to be sexually attracted to your partner (unless sexual attraction is something you don't feel in general). I'm not saying dismiss your superficial preferences altogether. I'm saying that attraction can be present even when someone is not ticking *every* box on your list. You're settling when the attraction isn't present whatsoever and is unable to grow – however, you're not settling when you're attracted to someone but they happen to be a little shorter than you would have preferred.

In my eyes, settling is choosing to be with someone who isn't as good as you deserve. It's being with someone who under-appreciates you. It's being with someone who makes you feel unhappy. It's being with someone who knows your boundaries but still disregards them. It's being with someone you're not attracted to whatsoever. It's being with someone you have to dim yourself for.

That's settling.

Not settling can be a lonely process

> *When you affirm that the people you allow into your life will need to have certain qualities, you automatically filter out people who don't meet the standard. This could lead to filtering a lot of people out. On your journey to setting standards and not settling, you have to be willing to walk alone longer than you may have typically done in the past.*

Setting a good standard for potential partners may seem like a relatively straight forward process on paper. But the truth is, it's not as easy as it may appear. People often assume that the only work involved is outlining a list of positive qualities we want in someone, and only entertaining a person if they have said qualities. Indeed, this is part of the process, but there's more work to it. Setting a standard while dating requires security, courage, willpower and faith.

When I began setting thorough standards for myself and asserting my non-negotiables, I began to realise how important it was for me to love my own company. You need to love your own company, otherwise when you are alone, you can easily end up looking for just anybody to fill the space open for a companion. Loving your own company means only wanting someone to fill the space when they have value to add.

With this said, as much as I grew to love my own company, I also realised that feeling lonely sometimes was absolutely normal. When you're setting standards for the kind of partner you want in your life, you will feel lonely on occasion, but it's what you do in your moments of loneliness that makes all the difference. Do you dismiss your non-negotiables for the sake of companionship or do you remind yourself that the solitude you are experiencing is an active choice – made by you, for you?

Finding a partner isn't difficult if you have zero standards and requirements. There are endless lists of people across the world who would happily jump at the opportunity to be with you. What is difficult is finding the *right* kind of partner for you. To find them, you need to be secure enough that you aren't in search of a partner for validation. Because when you are searching for validation, you will give away the space meant for someone who is good for you – to someone who is simply just 'there'. When we experience insecurities or trauma, we tend to look to others to validate us in some way and in the search for validation, it can become easy for us to let people into our lives where they really shouldn't be taking up space.

The self-love that helps us foster positive relationship experiences also gives us the willpower to say 'no' to what is not serving our needs. It gives us the strength to decide we're not going to let people into our life if they are not delivering the kind of love we desire and deserve. Self-love also gives us the faith to say, 'I know I'm going to find what I am looking for', and the courage to assert that 'it may take some time and I may be alone for a little while, but I can handle it and the wait will be worth it'.

As I write this book, I want to deliver the bitter truths with the sweet ones. I don't want to deceive you into thinking dating when you love yourself is always going to be sugar and spice and everything nice. Sometimes it may not always feel nice. When you love yourself, you choose yourself, which means not choosing people who will encourage you to dismiss your values and needs. But choosing yourself *can* feel lonely. You may even question your own decisions when you choose yourself. You may ask: 'why the hell am I doing this? Everyone else is in a relationship but I'm not.' You may feel like disregarding some of your non-negotiables because you're scared of being alone. But recognise that the loneliness hurdle will be worth it when you find someone who delivers the kind of qualities you deserve.

Always choose yourself and fight through the loneliness.

Look out for green flags just as much as red ones

Sometimes we can be so preoccupied with looking out for warning signs which suggest a person is bad for us, that we may overlook positive signs which suggest the opposite. By all means, be vigilant when it comes to spotting potential danger, but also look out for potential safety.

One thing I have noticed about discussions surrounding relationships is how easy it can be to talk about the nega- tives. Heartache and heartbreak have a long-lasting and unforgettable impact on us, so it's unsurprising that many of us focus on the not-so-positive aspects of past and current experiences when we're talking about love. This might be why when people discuss what to look out for in the early stages of dating, 'red flags' are often at the forefront of their minds. Red flags highlight danger. When we're talking about them in the context of a rela- tionship, a red flag signifies that a person may be bad for us. But what about the opposite? Green flags are also important.

A few examples of green flags include people who can handle conflict maturely and amicably, people who are clear and consistent about their intentions, people who respect others around them (including those they have nothing to gain from), people who listen to understand, people who respect your time, people who don't gaslight you or invalidate your feelings and many more.

Green flags make all the difference and it's very important that we train ourselves to understand and spot them. One way to do this is to write a list which details character traits you would like to see in a partner, then in a second column, detail behaviour that signifies this character trait. For example, if you would like a partner who considers your feelings, then one way they may demonstrate this trait is by actively listening to you when you open up – making 'someone who is an active listener' a green flag.

Safeguarding ourselves from potential danger is an important thing to do, but we should also be able to acknowledge positive behaviour in people. Also, an absence of obvious red flags doesn't automatically make someone a potentially great partner for you. I think the presence of green flags is just as important.

Don't forget to work on being the best version of yourself

> *When dating, we can sometimes focus so heavily on what other people are bringing to the table, without considering what we are delivering. It's no use looking for someone who is great for you while you're presenting the worst version of yourself.*

When I was planning this book, I told myself that one thing I didn't want to do was eradicate responsibility or accountability. I didn't want to eradicate the role we all play in our own love lives. When we're meeting people, sometimes we can be so consumed with how they should behave, how they should act, how they should think, etc., without considering the qualities we present to them.

Let's do a quick exercise ... I want you to write down some of your favourite qualities and characteristics in yourself. Write as much as you want to. For example, if you're a really thoughtful gift giver, include that. If you're non-judgemental and easy to talk to, include that. If you're trustworthy and reliable, include that. Write whatever comes to mind.

Once you have outlined your favourite characteristics, consider your least favourite. In my case, I can be quite petty with my words when I feel threatened. I can also be a bit impatient at times, and I show frustration when things aren't going my way. I'm not the most proactively affectionate person either. I'm affectionate when someone shows me affection but I don't always consider showing it first. I can also be incredibly proud and withhold vulnerability that could benefit my relationships, purely because I don't want to be on the back foot.

I'm sharing this with you to highlight the importance of knowing your strengths, weaknesses, good traits and flaws when entering relationships. I don't believe you need to be 'perfect' to be in a relationship, because frankly, who is? However, an awareness of the things you need to work on is important, and once you become aware of these less favourable traits, it is even more important to make an active effort to manage or eliminate them.

Don't lose your authentic self

> *When dating, many people are focused on 'impressing' the people they're meeting. Nothing is wrong with wanting to make a good first impression but it should never be at the expense of displaying your authentic self. Your goal is to find someone who appreciates you, for you.*

A common mistake people make when dating is trying too hard to impress. Some people try so hard that they become inauthentic. They present a version of themselves that is largely inaccurate, because they question whether they will be appreciated as their authentic self. When I say this, I'm not talking purely about what's on the surface. So yes, while borrowing your friend's car or wearing a push up bra may seem 'inauthentic' to some, I'm speaking about character, personality and behaviour.

Have I ever done this? Most definitely. When I was younger I told some white lies about my cooking skills and interest in sport. Which, for the most part, can be considered harmless. But I've also participated in the type of inauthenticity that is a lot more harmful. The type that involved downplaying my needs, and diminishing aspects of my personality that define who I am, because I didn't want to come across 'too serious', or 'too independent', or 'too outspoken' or 'too confident'.

With age I learned some very important things. The wrong person will like you for who you are pretending to be. The right person will like you for who you are. You do yourself a disservice when you present a diluted version of yourself to other people. It's also a disservice to the person you are dating, because you remove the opportunity for them to get to know the real you. Presenting an inaccurate version of yourself also becomes very tiring and frustrating in the long term. If you do build a relationship based on a façade, you will feel pressure to keep the façade up, and while 'pretending' on day one may feel easy and harmless, keeping up the pretense can do real damage to your wellbeing and your relationship. It's also an easy way for you to build resentment for the other person, because if they do eventually get access to the real you and they don't like it, you will grow to dislike them and dislike yourself.

SECTION 1: THE DATING STAGE

When dating, we can feel so much pressure to 'impress' but impressing shouldn't be the real priority. The real priority should always be getting to know people in an open and honest way, while also presenting ourselves in an open and honest way.

Having a life outside of your love life is essential

Relationships work out better when each person has a productive life outside of their relationship. If your relationship is your life and your life is your relationship, you're in for trouble. A healthy relationship should complement your life, not become it.

When I was in my late teens and early twenties, I made the common mistake of abandoning my social life and aspirations whenever I entered a relationship. When I had a boyfriend, I went out less, lost focus and deprioritised myself – as well as my dreams and goals. I tried to play the role of 'supportive girlfriend', and, in my mind, that meant putting myself last in every way.

This is something plenty of women have done at some point in their life – and some men too. Although, I do think this behaviour is more common among women for a variety of reasons. In patriarchal social systems, in which men hold the power, women are viewed as subordinates who only really have value when they are desired by men or connected to a man through a relationship. As a young girl, when you are constantly bombarded with depictions of heterosexual women prioritising marriage or the men in their life, it becomes very easy to do the same (even when the man in your life never asked you to prioritise him). I fell victim to this narrative and it affected me and my relationships in harmful ways.

In my mind, being supportive involved centring my partner in everything. I treated myself as if I mattered less than the relationship, which was a massive mistake on my part.

A partner who is good for you, wants you to flourish and wants you to be the best version of yourself. The best version of yourself is well-rounded, and to be well-rounded, one should have friendships outside of their romantic relationship, hobbies outside of their romantic relationship and aspirations outside of their relationship. Also, while we would love all relationships to stand the test of time, the truth is … most don't. I'm not being negative when I share this, just factual. Having a life outside of your romantic relationship is an essential insurance policy. When you make your partner your life, and your life your partner, what happens if the relation-ship ends and you break up? I'll tell you what happens. You'll feel like you've lost everything. It's also harder for you to heal because you've rid yourself of the activities and friendships you once had which would have helped you move on from the breakup. Alongside trying to manage the feelings associated with the breakup, you'll be forced to rebuild the life you once had – which makes everything much harder.

Do not abandon your life for love, and anyone who truly loves you won't want you to anyway.

You will always appear needy to someone who isn't giving you enough

> *There are many people who aren't naturally 'needy' but they are mislabelled as needy because they are not being given the care and attention they deserve.*

Have you ever been called 'needy' before? Perhaps you craved a person's attention in an excessive way because you have been abandoned by people in the past, and that made you anxious? Perhaps you desired the constant company of others because you didn't enjoy your own company? Perhaps you looked to people for constant validation because you had low self-esteem? The source of an excessive 'need' for emotional support is often trauma based. It occurs because something happened *to* you.

However, there is another type of behaviour which is labelled as 'needy', but actually isn't needy at all. It is the type of behaviour that emerges when someone is failing to give you the bare minimum. It's the type of behaviour that is a result of people feeling frustrated and under-appreciated.

When we are in relationships and we are treated like a second thought or even a burden, we end up wanting 'more' from our partner. We want more on the basis that what we are receiving is not enough – not because we want too much, but because what we are receiving is unsatisfactory.

People who provide a typically unsatisfactory amount of attention and care in a relationship, will always consider bare minimum requests to be 'needy'. If you find yourself in a relationship which is making you appear needy, ask yourself why. Did your behaviour emerge at the start of the relationship or did it worsen with time? Does your partner's behaviour exacerbate a feeling of frustration? Are you in a state of permanent anxiety that you have carried throughout all your previous relationships or does all of this feel new?

If you come to the conclusion that your partner's lack of commitment and involvement is unsatisfactory and bringing out a side of you that you have never seen before, communicate this to them. If they're unwilling to give you the time and effort you require, ask yourself if that is the kind of relationship you want.

We don't own people, we experience them

> *Your partner does not belong to you. They are not yours to own. They are yours to experience.*

In 2019, the world lost Ermias Joseph Asghedom – also known as rapper Nipsey Hussle. His passing broke the hearts of people across the globe, including his partner at the time, actress Lauren London. In a moving speech after his death, Lauren mentioned that Nipsey once told her: 'you can't possess people, you can only experience them', and I'll never forget that. It reminded me of another quote with a similar message, shared by Indian mystic, Osho: 'If you love a flower, don't pick it up. Because if you pick it up it ceases to be what you love. So if you love a flower, let it be. Love is not about possession. Love is about appreciation.' Admittedly, Osho is viewed as a very controversial mystic, but this quote does a good job of capturing the message I'm hoping to relay. This message is one about possession, and how society often normalises possession within relationships.

Many people are of the opinion that they 'own' their partner. They believe the person they are romantically connected to is theirs and nobody else's. The problem there is that your partner does indeed belong to one person – themselves. *They* control who they are connected to, what they do and what they don't do. There is also a big difference between love and possession. When we possess people, we centre ourselves in their lives. We think they are responsible for making us happy. When we love people, we want them to centre themselves in their own lives. We understand that we are responsible for making ourselves happy and we do not place the responsibility on them. When we possess people, we are jealous of the relationships they have with others. When we love them, we understand that it's normal and healthy for people to have a social network. When we possess people, we want to dominate them and control them. When we love people, we understand that they have their own views, opinions and desires, and we respect their differences. We don't own people, we experience them.

Now before I go on, I want to stress that experiencing people isn't an excuse for them to cause you hurt or harm. I don't want this lesson to be misinterpreted. Experiencing people doesn't mean you should tolerate what goes against your boundaries or what falls into your non-negotiables. Relationships are about respecting one another, after all. Stripping ownership away simply helps to emphasise that everyone is an individual, with their own thoughts and lives outside their relationship.

Understanding that you are experiencing people also helps to reduce negative emotions like jealousy. This is because through understanding that you do not own people, you also come to understand that they are entitled to experience the world how they wish to, and you are also less likely to take things personally when they do. Mutual respect (which includes respecting non-negotiables) is important in relationships, but people are very capable of respecting your non-negotiables while taking ownership over their own lives and having autonomy over their own minds and bodies.

Your partner is not yours to own in life. They are a companion you enjoy life with.

People express and receive love differently

Finding out about 'love languages' really transformed the way I view love. I stopped assessing love through my own lens and, instead, accepted the fact that some people love differently to me. Instead of assuming how people like to be loved, I let them tell me. This has made me more understanding and my relationships with others more harmonious.

The Five Love Languages is a book published by author, speaker and counsellor Dr Gary Chapman. In this world-renowned book, Chapman outlines five ways people typically like to receive love and express it. The five 'love languages' outlined in Dr Chapman's book include quality time, acts of service, physical touch, giving gifts and words of affirmation.

Before reading this book, I had never truly considered the role love languages play in our relationships with others. I had never really stopped to consider the fact two people can have a relationship (whether that's friendship, familial or romantic) and express their love to each other in two completely different ways.

The reason I even read the book in the first place is because my parents were going through a rough patch when I was in my early twenties, and part of their healing process included reading this book (after being advised to by a relationship counsellor). They soon discovered that despite the fact they had been married for over twenty years at the time, they expressed love and liked to receive love in completely different ways. This mismatch meant that prior to reading this book, they sometimes felt as if they weren't being loved adequately by one another. When in reality, part of their frustration was due to expressing love in a way that wasn't necessarily appreciated by their partner.

To break it down more simply, you may feel as if someone is showing you they love you when they spend their weekends with you (quality time) and hold your hand often (physical touch). Meanwhile, your partner may rarely do this – not because they don't love you but because they love when a person runs errands for them (acts of service) and compliments them daily (words of affirmation). They may be expressing their love in a way they appreciate and understand, but because their prominent love languages are different to yours, you end up feeling unloved at times.

It's very easy for us to assume that people 'love' in the exact same way we do. I assumed this a lot when I was in my twenties, and would end up very frustrated with partners, even in my happiest relationship. I would question why things that were important to me weren't as important to them. I would query why I had to request for certain things to happen, and why they wouldn't just occur 'naturally'. When I learned about love languages, so much began to make sense.

My advice to everyone is to either read the *Five Love Languages* book or take a love languages quiz online, and don't forget to ask your loved ones to take it too. I know my sister's love language, the love languages my parents use and my brother's. Love languages aren't limited to romantic relationships. We all like being loved differently. Also, I think it's important to highlight that love languages can change. What you may prioritise now, may not be what you prioritise ten years from now. For example, your top love language in your twenties may be quality time, but in your forties it may be acts of service. Be aware of the changes in you and changes in your

relationships which may influence a change in your love
language.

Uncomfortable conversations are often required for comfortable relationships

Certain conversations aren't easy to have but they are necessary, and sometimes the only thing standing between growth, healing and understanding is an uncomfortable conversation.

Earlier in this chapter, I mentioned that I had an uncomfortable conversation with my dad when I was 31. It was a conversation that pulled out a lot of buried feelings and experiences, but it was also a conversation that pulled us closer together.

In any type of relationship – whether it's with a friend, family member or lover – it can be very difficult to initiate certain types of conversation. These conversations may include ways the relationship isn't working well, bringing up the past to discuss how it has shaped the present, taking accountability for doing something wrong or sharing something that could hurt the other person.

I've been in relationships that required uncomfortable conversations but I skated around them because I couldn't bring myself to confront the fact something was wrong. I wanted to live in a bubble and pretend that all was well. I also didn't want to risk the potential of triggering something that was much worse. In my mind the conversation could only go one way – and that was badly. Adding to that, I was also concerned about coming across ungrateful, unappreciative or like a nag. So at the end of the day, I didn't have the conversations, which led to the breakdown of relationships or me hurting people anyway.

After reflecting on how my unwillingness to be open impacted things, I began speaking up more. I immediately noticed that uncomfortable conversations lead to short term pain, but long term gain. In the moment they can be tough, painful, emotional and heart-wrenching, but many of us are walking around with a weight on our shoulders that needs to be eased. All of my uncomfortable conversations lifted weight, which led to me carrying less frustration and resentment in the relationship. It's like therapy. If you've ever spoken to a therapist before you would know that it can be scary. It can open you up to the fact you are living with unresolved issues, but once you get past the initial hurdle of opening up and unpacking the weight you are carrying, you begin to feel lighter and more at peace – which makes your life easier and happier in the long run.

Uncomfortable conversations can help people understand us better. They can help us change our perspective. They can help us grow as people. They can help us heal from the past, mend bonds, build bonds and so much more. They're important to have and not run away from.

With this said, part of having a productive uncomfortable conversation is having it in an effective way. I've made the mistake of thinking if a conversation topic is uncomfortable, it doesn't matter how I say it or when I say it, because at the end of the day the topic is a difficult one to discuss anyway. But I was wrong. Just because a conversation topic is uncomfortable doesn't mean we shouldn't try to have it in a comfortable way. And while you may think there is never a 'right' time, that doesn't mean some times aren't better than others. When I want to have difficult conversations now, I always think about the when and how: when will I say it and how will I say it. It's helpful when two people can talk at a time when they are both as relaxed as they can be. It's also helpful to be compassionate with your honesty. Don't lie, but don't be nasty about the truth. Even if the other person believes you are saying the wrong thing, you can still say it in the right way.

Lastly, another aspect of having a productive conversation is talking to someone who is willing to listen. Sadly, the productivity of conversations isn't always in our hands. We could say and do everything in the best way possible, but if the other person isn't willing to listen, that presents another challenge …

Good communication is not just about talking

The topic of being a good communicator can often heavily revolve around speaking but there are other important qualities that are needed. Can you be vulnerable? Are you in tune with your emotions? Can you speak calmly amid conflict? You can be a great speaker in many ways, but if you are unable to listen to others, you aren't a good communicator.

I used to be a terrible listener, particularly during emotional moments and times of crisis. I was just awful. I was the listener who listened to reply, instead of to understand. I was often too busy developing a rebuttal in my mind that I didn't even absorb what the other person was saying. I would regularly hear what I wanted to hear, and would conveniently disregard the bits that wouldn't suit my rebuttal. It wasn't pretty. Despite this, I regarded myself as a good communicator because I was so willing to have discussions and I often received compliments for being very articulate. But being a good communicator is a two-way street; it involves speaking *and* listening. I know this now more than ever, but in my early twenties I didn't.

My issues with communication didn't do me any favours on the relationship front. In times of disagreement, I would often replay a very different conversation in my mind because of my inability to adequately listen. My rebuttals would reflect my feelings instead of what the other person was saying. I would interject before the other person had even finished talking and arguments would last a lot longer than necessary because my listening was poor.

On the flip side, I've dated people who were great listeners and awful talkers. They could listen to me talk about my emotions 'til kingdom come but getting them to be vulnerable and open was a struggle. I imagine that struggle must have been heightened as it's hard to be vulnerable with someone who isn't doing a great job of listening …

Part of my own journey towards becoming a better partner and person in general was working on my communication skills on the listening front. I've developed a few steps to help me become a better listener, and I want to share these steps with you.

The first step is to allow two seconds of silence before replying to others. This can help us to listen better because it discourages us from jumping straight into a rebuttal. Although short, that two-second pause gives us a moment to consider how we want to approach the next stage of our discussion.

The second step is to stop planning your responses in your mind. When we are in conversation with a person and we are planning our response as they are speaking, we can easily end up losing track of what they are saying because we are focusing more on what *we* want to say. This step is succinctly summarised by author and educator, Stephen R. Covey, in his bestselling book *The 7 Habits of Highly Effective People*. In Covey's words, 'most people do not listen with the intent to understand; they listen with the intent to reply'. A massive part of being a better listener is worrying less about your response and, instead, listening to understand.

Another important step for me was slowing down my speaking. This may not be relevant to you if you are generally a slow speaker anyway, but I am not. When I get going, I speak quickly and when nervous or stressed,

I can often say much more than I actually should. Slowing down your speaking can help you become a better listener because it gives you time to really consider what you've just heard as you respond. When you talk quickly, you are often more preoccupied with all the thoughts in your head, rather than directly touching on the messages that were shared with you.

My last step involves breathing and volume control. Steady breathing is an important part of effective communication that people rarely consider. Fast paced and shallow breaths are indicative of anxiousness. They in turn make people feel even more nervous, and nervousness doesn't support productive listening. Learning to control your breathing can help you calm yourself, which improves the way you approach conversations. My tips for good breathing while talking include taking a deep breath through your nose before you start to speak. This will help to relax you initially. Monitoring your breath as it flows through your lungs and out your mouth is also important as many people forget to breathe altogether when they're nervous. Be aware of the tension in your body – relaxing your shoulders and unclenching your jaw will also help you to breathe more effectively. Volume control is also important for listening because people often increase their volume in tense and emotionally driven situations. Speaking at top volume can encourage your brain to process the discussion as an attack. Attacks make us defensive and defensiveness can limit our ability to listen. Controlling your volume helps to remind you that you're engaging in a discussion that is supposed to be productive, as opposed to a heated and unproductive argument.

Once you improve your listening, you will begin to notice that your conversations will display improved understanding, closeness and even more value.

Focus on the journey

> *You break your own heart when you create your ideal ending and focus on that instead of focusing on the actual journey.*

Have you ever found yourself daydreaming about your future with someone? Perhaps you imagined your future home, your children, your wedding. Maybe you even went a step further and found yourself obsessing over these ideal scenarios? To the point that you ended up creating goals for yourself – goals that consumed all your attention?

I've certainly done this. In a past relationship I placed so much emphasis on what I was hoping to get out of it that what I put into it was largely connected to what I hoped would be the end result. I know that I'm not alone too. Many of my friends have gone above and beyond when dating a man because their ideal ending was to be in a committed relationship with him; only for them to unknowingly dilute their authentic selves because they were more focused on the ending than the journey.

When we focus too much on an ideal ending, we do ourselves a disservice. We can often find ourselves struggling to enjoy the present, because we are too engrossed in the future. We can find ourselves spoiling our journey because we're placing too much emphasis on our ideal ending. We can find ourselves comparing our relationship with other relationships because the external journey holds more weight than our personal experience. We can find ourselves feeling resentful when our ideal ending doesn't manifest. We can find ourselves behaving inauthentically because we're focused too much on achieving a goal and not enough on actually getting to know someone for who they are and not who we want them to be. We can find ourselves placing unnecessary and unhelpful timelines on things we should simply enjoy. We can find ourselves giving people ultimatums or difficult choices, simply because we're the ones in a rush to achieve an ideal ending for ourselves. We can find ourselves judging situations and people incorrectly, because we're so desperate to manifest what we have set our heart on. We can find ourselves making hasty and unwise decisions because we are rushing when we should be slowing down.

When it comes to romantic relationships, I think it's helpful to have an end goal in mind to a degree. After all, it helps to know where you're headed and being intentional leaves less room for problems. However, problems can easily arise when we fail to strike a balance. End goals are important but don't be so lost in them that you fail to properly assess and enjoy the present. Enjoy getting to know people. Enjoy learning with them, growing with them, discovering with them, embarking on new experiences with them.

Sometimes we won't reach our ideal ending but when we learn to enjoy the journey, we can reflect on the experience happily. The time we invested is less likely to trigger regret, because we actually enjoyed the time and chose to invest it willingly, based on how we felt day by day.

See people for who they are and allow the present to shape your end goal. Give yourself permission to enjoy your journeys.

Set a standard by the way you treat yourself

> *Treat yourself with the utmost care and respect. When people see that you set a high standard for yourself, they're more inclined to provide a higher standard for you. Never dim yourself in an attempt to attract a partner.*

I'm all for people not downplaying themselves in an attempt to find a partner. Sadly, too many of us do it – particularly women. Plenty of women downplay themselves because they don't want to come across as 'intimidating' or 'high-maintenance' when dating. The thing is, these adjectives are often used to describe women who know exactly how they want to be treated in relationships, and won't settle for less. What I have come to learn from women who are often given these labels, is that for the most part, people treat you according to the standard you set and showcase for yourself. Plenty 'intimidating' and 'high-maintenance' women command respect, and they treat themselves with the utmost care and respect as a way of demonstrating that. They present the best version of themselves and they wear their strengths and achievements proudly, and at the end of the day, they attract people who admire those strengths and achievements.

Will certain people be intimidated by the best version of you? Most definitely. You *will* intimidate some people. But the ones you intimidate aren't the ones you should want to be with anyway. When someone is intimidated by your strengths, it makes for a fragile relationship and what you need is a partner who feels confident and comfortable enough to be with you. Don't dim yourself in an attempt to attract a partner. It's never worth it. Always be your authentic and brilliant self, and set a standard for yourself. In doing so, you filter out plenty of the people who cannot deliver that standard.

'But how do I set a standard for myself?' is one question I get asked often. Setting a standard for yourself is often linked to money and materialism, and while being seen to spend money on yourself is one form, it's definitely the least important. Beyond the superficial side of setting standards, consider how you treat yourself.

Ways you can set a standard for yourself include:

- Respecting your own boundaries
- Going where you are celebrated and not just tolerated
- Setting aside time for yourself and not centring other people in everything that you do
- Speaking your mind
- Trusting your opinions
- Holding your head high when walking and talking
- Prioritising your wellbeing and not jeopardising it to cater to others
- Speaking highly of yourself and not putting yourself down
- Being proud of your achievements
- Treating people with respect and compassion

When other people see that you set a standard for yourself and that you are confident with it, people who complement that will gravitate towards you. Might you still attract people who aren't good for you? Yes (sadly that's unavoidable), but you will filter out a great deal of these people. You will also encourage yourself to navigate your relationships in a way that benefits you and works for you, instead of just your partner.

Before I made the decision to set a standard for myself, I would tolerate a lot of negative behaviour. I also entered relationships as a passenger and never really worked in partnership to steer the direction. I behaved as if I was secondary to my partner and would rarely speak my mind in regards to my needs and wants. I didn't approach relationships as if I was important. When I realised this and did the self-work to implement changes in the way I view myself and the relationships in my life, I began having more fulfilling relationships that worked for me instead of relationships that I constantly had to work for. My partner selection process also focused heavily on the value *they* brought to the relationship, not just the value I brought. I realised that I am deserving of good things and had to be good to myself first and foremost. I realised that I didn't need to 'audition' for relationships. I just needed to be unapologetically me.

Section 2:
The Loving Stage

Oh to love and be loved. What a wonderful feeling. Arguably the best feeling. Not much can compare. Whether it's the love of your friends, family or romantic partner. Love in general is something that ties us all together and despite how 'whole' we feel without it, the presence of love in our life reminds us that we will never feel more whole than when we love ourselves and we are loved by someone else – no matter who that someone is.

With this said, love can also be frightening because it comes with risks. Whether it's the risk your love will be unrequited, the risk your heart will be broken or the risk you grow so madly and deeply in love that you cannot fathom an existence without the other person – which is an overwhelming thought. Giving your heart to someone is no easy feat, but in life, most rewards come with an element of risk. Despite the risks involved, human beings choose to love every day, because for many people, the potential rewards in love greatly outweigh the potential risks. Even after being hurt and telling ourselves we will love no more, we often still gravitate towards the possibility of love because it's what makes us human.

In this section of my book, I want to share love lessons that I learned through taking my own risks, and learning through love.

Love is a choice

> *Romantic love isn't something that 'happens' to you. It is a decision you make. It is something you are in control of. When you realise love is a choice that is guided by you, you begin to start making better choices and decisions. You can choose to love people who value you and who are good to you.*

Throughout history we have been presented with the notion that people 'fall in love'. The depiction of Cupid is a prime example of this. In Roman mythology, Cupid is the winged son of Venus (the goddess of love). Depictions of Cupid in modern media present us with a sweet looking innocent baby (or cherub) flying through the skies, holding a magical bow and arrows that possess the power to unleash uncontrollable lust and infatuation in anyone an arrow strikes.

For a long time I believed real love wasn't too dissimilar. I believed that we as human beings didn't possess the power to choose who we fell in love with. We just kind of … fell. I believed that love was an uncontrollable emotion and that if you didn't feel those emotions quickly with someone, then the possibility of them emerging was impossible.

However, I soon learned through a series of observations and experiences, that buying into this narrative was unhelpful and at times dangerous to our romantic lives. To assess how it can be harmful and unhelpful, we first need to acknowledge that as humans, what we are attracted to is influenced by our experiences – and not all of us have had great experiences. As an example, if you are a heterosexual woman with a father who is fairly emotionally unavailable, you may find yourself being attracted to this type of man. You may find yourself 'falling in love' with this type of man, not because he is good for you, but because he feels familiar, and what feels familiar often feels safe (even when it isn't). If we accept the notion that love is an uncontrollable feeling and not a choice, this means a woman with this habit and experience is somewhat destined to be bonded to emotionally unavailable men. This means she has no control of her romantic life or her outcomes beyond what she 'feels' internally.

This is why I rebuke the belief that love is an uncontrollable feeling and accept the belief that love is in fact, a choice.

Kiersten White is a *New York Times* bestselling author, and below is an excerpt from her novel *The Chaos of the Stars*:

> I didn't fall in love with you. I walked into love with you, with my eyes wide open, choosing to take every step along the way. I do believe in fate and destiny, but I also believe we are only fated to do the things that we'd choose anyway. And I'd choose you; in a hundred lifetimes, in a hundred worlds, in any version of reality, I'd find you and I'd choose you.

I love this excerpt. I love it because to me, this is what love should be. Not something we fall or tumble into, but something we actively *walk* into. Something we choose. The element of choice is very important because the feelings we often associate with being 'in love' can be fleeting. Feelings of lust, feelings of passion, feelings of infatuation. As I write this book, I'm not married, but one thing I do know through my personal observations of married couples (including my parents who have been married for more than thirty years) is that the feeling of infatuation, lust and passion often disappear and reappear. But what defines their love for each other is the choices they make every day, and those choices become actions. Whether it's a choice to remain committed, a choice to put their best foot forward, a choice to be loyal, a choice to be supportive … Their love is depicted in their choices and in turn their behaviours – not simply their 'feelings'.

Love more than just potential

> *It's beautiful when we can see the best in people. It's wonderful when we can recognise the potential in others. But when it comes to choosing to love someone, it's unhelpful when we value their 'potential' more than their present reality.*

Have you ever fallen for someone's 'potential' before? I certainly have. I found myself creating a picture in my head of who they were that wasn't completely accurate. The picture wasn't accurate because it was based largely on what I believed they were capable of and not what they were actually doing. This led to me feeling frustrated within the relationship. By the end of the relationship I felt as if I had fallen for someone I didn't really recognise. I felt like they had behaved in a way which had surprised me. I felt as if they had done things that I didn't think were in their nature. When I asked myself why I stayed for as long as I did, it was because I focused heavily on the 'potential future' we could have together, without considering how we were connecting as a couple in the present.

The truth of the matter was that I hadn't been surprised or bamboozled by my partner; everything they did was natural to them, but I had focused so much on their positive potential that I had almost created an imaginary person in my mind. I was so blinded by their potential that I even dismissed things I would consider to be amber flags, because they didn't mirror up with the person I wanted them to be – and I saw them for who I wanted them to be, not who they truly were.

While I believe it's normal and healthy to *consider* a person's future potential when it comes to dating them, the mistake many people make is obsessing over it. Potential shouldn't be why we choose to love people. We should choose to love people for who they really are because the painful truth is that potential doesn't always manifest. You may think a person is capable of moving mountains for you, but should those mountains never be moved, how will you feel? Also, when you fall for potential, you don't allow yourself the privilege of getting to really know the person right in front of you. Falling for potential is not just a disservice to you but it's also a disservice to the person you are choosing to love.

Signs you may love the *idea* of someone more than you love them as a person, include:

- Focusing heavily on the future instead of the present
- Regularly thinking about the 'potential' that they have yet to reach
- Focusing most on their superficial qualities
- Dismissing their flaws or making excuses for them

Falling in love with 'potential', can be a slippery slope. You end up dismissing the reality in front of you and falling for a possible future that hasn't even manifested, and may never come to pass. The love you invest in someone is contingent on them changing who they currently are to become a 'better version' that lives in your head. But the thing is ... We don't possess the power to change people. People change because *they* want to.

Believing we possess the power to change people is problematic. Many people who believe they have this power enter relationships with the knowledge that the other person is unable to give them the kind of partnership they desire in the moment. They overlook this glaring issue because they have convinced themselves the other person's problems are theirs to conquer. Infatuation can make people behave in this way.

Another reason one may behave in this way is trauma linked to the past. Sometimes it's not that people believe they have the power to change others, but that they *hope* they are able to, as an attempt to heal an old wound. Perhaps a caregiver or guardian from their childhood had a specific negative quality and that quality deeply hurt them. An inability to change a person in the past may leave someone with a desire to change a person in the present – and 'fix' a behaviour in someone they couldn't fix as a child.

If you recognise this behaviour in yourself, I recommend speaking to a professional about it. If your access to a therapist is limited, perhaps a counsellor can help you explore the aspects of your past that play a role in the people you are drawn to. One thing I discovered through my own discussions with a therapist is that we cannot love people into being good for us.

You can love someone to the moon and back but just because you love them doesn't mean they are capable of loving you properly in that moment. Your love can't make a person good for you. Your love won't fulfil their potential.

If you've fallen for potential before, you've likely felt like you loved someone immensely, but found yourself feeling frustrated because they just couldn't be the person you needed them to be for you. Maybe in an attempt to help them, you loved them even harder, but no matter what, things didn't change …

Sometimes we can assume that if we give someone 110 per cent, they will be who we need them to be, but this simply isn't the case. Although a relationship takes two, people still present as individuals with their own independent minds, thoughts and feelings. While we have the ability to influence what goes through people's heads, we cannot control it. So please be mindful of this, before making the decision to enter a relationship based solely on a person's potential.

Struggle is not a rite of passage we must experience before happiness

> *Despite what some people may lead you to believe, struggle is not an essential part of being in a loving relationship and you don't need to prove you can 'handle' struggle to be deserving of loyalty and care.*

I'm ashamed to say that once upon a time I thought I had to tolerate struggle to prove I am deserving of love. If you've heard the term 'ride or die chick' before, there's a chance you know exactly what I'm talking about. I thought I had to be *that* girlfriend. The type to forgive my partner for all their indiscretions and 'hold them down' through struggle and strife, no matter what. I thought I had to put my needs and wellbeing on the back-burner to support my relationship in any way I could. I felt as if experiencing hardship in a relationship was 'normal' and that 'ups and downs' were to be expected and accepted. How silly and naïve I was. But we learn, and we move.

As a 30-something-year-old woman, I am proud to say I now understand that loving someone through the 'ups and downs' should be challenges you face together – not challenges you face alone because your partner doesn't respect you. I now wholeheartedly rebuke the idea of 'struggle love'. Struggle love being the belief that a person (typically a woman), must face hardship, struggle, heartache and stress before ultimately experiencing a peaceful and harmonious relationship or 'happy ending'.

The glorification of struggle love is one I have witnessed in music, television, film and in my own community, and I'm sure this played a massive role in convincing me that it's something I had to experience to be happy … eventually. Whenever I witnessed struggle love, it always involved a receiver and an offender – someone who was expected to tolerate the struggle and someone who causes problems. The struggle never came from both parties and 100 per cent of the time, the receiver was a woman.

The struggle love narrative is extremely harmful for a number of reasons. When we suggest to people that struggle must be experienced before love, we are telling them that it's unrealistic to experience an immediately loving and healthy relationship, absent of chaos and conflict. When we suggest to people that struggle must be experienced before love, we are excusing negative and abusive behaviour and treating it as if it is a 'normal' part of a relationship journey. When we suggest to people that struggle must be experienced before love, we are saying that love is to be earned after testing a person's willingness to accept less than what they deserve. When we suggest to people that struggle must be experienced before love, we are setting a damaging precedent – creating relationships absent of equal respect and effort.

When I reflect on my own experiences with struggle love, I take responsibility for accepting certain things because I didn't feel deserving or valuable. I felt like I had to prove my value and confirm to the other person that they had made a good decision by 'choosing me'. And my way of doing that was through accepting less, saying less and becoming less of a person than I truly was. In my mind, if I did all that, they would think I was wonderful – but that's not what happened. And I'm thankful.

Want to know what happened? Eventually I tolerated so much disrespect that the relationship felt meaningless to me. I had turned into a robot – totally numb to their harmful behaviours – and that made me realise there was a problem. I eventually summoned up the courage to walk away, and when I did, I realised that during the relationship I had internalised struggle love. I had internalised the belief that love had to be earned by me (a woman) through enduring pain and hardship alongside a man. In hindsight I realised that I allowed myself to judge my partner differently to how I judged myself. I held a high standard for my behaviour, and a low standard for him, because I thought it was my duty at the time to tolerate his indiscretions in order to sustain the relationship, make him a better person, and prove my value.

I have since realised that I do not have to endure hardship to be deserving of love and respect, and that being a woman does not have to come with tolerating mistreatment at the hands of men just to be able to say that I am in a relationship.

Feelings are individual

> *You can't assume that the way you feel in your relationship is the same way your partner feels. Two people can be in a relationship yet feel two very different emotions and can even interpret the relationship in two completely different ways.*

When I entered my thirties, I was in a relationship with a lovely guy. It didn't work out because I had other priorities and didn't want to waste his time, but one thing he was great at doing was asking me how I *really* felt. The first time he did this was when we were in the early stages of dating, and the conversation went like this:

Him: 'How are you doing?'

Me: 'I'm fine, thanks. What about you?'

Him: 'I mean, how are you really doing?'

Me: 'Really doing? Why do you ask?'

Him: 'I just don't like assuming how the other
person feels. I'm doing great and I'm really
enjoying getting to know you, but I wanted to
make sure you're also happy with us, and just
overall.'

I was flabbergasted. I guess when he posed this question,
I had never really considered how easily people default to
'I'm fine' or 'I'm good' when we're asked how we feel. I
had also never really considered the fact 'feelings' aren't an
automatically shared experience when in a relationship.
For all he knew at the time, I could have been having an
awful experience getting to know him despite the fact he
was having a wonderful experience getting to know me.
Thankfully this wasn't the case, but I wanted to share my
own story to help you better understand this lesson.

Sometimes we can be so enthralled by our own
emotions that we don't take the time out to consider
how the other person is feeling. Many of us also rarely
entertain the idea that the person we're dating is having
a totally different experience to us, partly because the
thought of that can be a painful one. We're sometimes
quick to assume that they feel how we feel, but we
shouldn't be.

I think it's important in relationships (and when getting to know someone) to give each other the opportunity to communicate how they feel. A lot of people spend time talking about their day, their interests, where they should go, what they should eat, etc., without actually asking one another about their emotional, physical or mental state of being. On the occasions people do ask, it's often a blanket 'how are you?' without a real desire to know how the other person is *actually* feeling.

I think part of the reason we may not ask is out of fear or uneasiness. Sometimes we don't ask certain things because we are scared of the answer. Other times, we have an idea of what the answer may be but we don't ask because the thought of the next steps make us feel uneasy. Maybe we don't ask because we believe we are incapable of helping the other person through it effectively. Or we don't ask because we make the assumption that if something was wrong, the other person would automatically tell us. However, people tend to open up when they feel supported through the possibility. And part of supporting people through their vulnerability, is showing an interest in what they potentially have to say. Relationships are about partnership, and partnership comes with acknowledging that your partner has their own emotions, separate to yours. To form a fulfilling relationship, you both have a responsibility to explore each other's emotions – with compassion.

So moving forward, don't assume. Ask.

Pay attention to your gut

> We are all blessed with intuition, but, too
> often, we overlook it. This innate inclination,
> otherwise known as a 'gut feeling', is a bridge
> between our conscious and subconscious
> mind. Sometimes your subconscious mind is
> trying to tell you something that your
> conscious mind hasn't yet rationalised. Pay
> attention to it.

With age I have learned to trust my gut instinct, but I haven't always done this. When I was younger, I would have certain inclinations but would need reassurance from others. This would lead to me asking friends and family for their opinions, and then making decisions based on these external opinions, instead of how I truly felt.

I often hear people dismissing 'gut feelings' as some kind of pseudo-notion. It doesn't matter whether people label it as 'intuition', 'instinct' or a 'hunch', but it's rarely taken as seriously as people should take it. Maybe this is because people regard it as some kind of illogical psychic ability, but I actually believe there's a lot of logic involved in gut feelings, and the primal connection between our brain and our subconscious is there to protect us. In fact, my thoughts have been proven by a number of scientific journals whose research highlights that our brain's close relationship with our gut is powered by a range of neurons and hormones.

Through my own experiences, I've come to the belief that when we have a gut feeling, it's often guided by our subconscious mind. Our subconscious mind does an amazing job at processing things we aren't necessarily actively acknowledging. It could be that our subconscious mind has witnessed red flags we have overlooked or even pain we have buried. So what we call 'gut feelings' are actually logical feelings based on subconscious awareness or experience.

But how do we know that our gut feeling is exactly that, and not an attempt to sabotage something that is actually working well or force something that is actually working badly? How do we know it's a gut feeling and not a feeling caused by something else?

I think this goes back to our subconscious mind. We can attempt to communicate with it to determine the root of our feelings. Every time I have had a gut feeling, I've sat with it and asked myself what in the physical realm could be contributing to the feeling. Usually there are tangible occurrences or logical explanations. For example, I've had gut feelings that a previous partner was being unfaithful to me. In my head it was my 'woman's intuition' but in reality, I had noticed subtle changes in behaviour that I hadn't allowed myself to fully process. So what happened? These behavioural changes took home in my subconscious mind, and became a conscious thought once I began to consider what contributed to my gut feeling.

Often, when it comes to feelings linked to things like self-sabotage or our own relationship insecurities, there is either minimal evidence to support our feeling or there is contradictory evidence to disprove it.

Listen to your body. Pay attention to your gut and consider why it might be trying to communicate with you.

Controlling your ego is an important part of a relationship

Our ego can prevent us from saying what we really feel, apologising for our mistakes and taking accountability for our actions. It can also limit our growth by negatively impacting the way we take on constructive criticism. This is why learning to control your ego is one of the best things you can do for yourself and your relationships.

Sigmund Freud was an Austrian neurologist who termed the word 'ego' in 1923. Through his work on psychoanalysis, Freud defined ego as a mediator between the external real word and our internal personality. Ego, as defined by Freud, is our understanding of ourselves. The part of us which negotiates between who we truly are and the societal standards which we have become accustomed to. While critics of Freud have disputed certain parts of his understanding of our ego, one thing we do know for sure is that ego feeds our sense of self. And many of us commonly understand the word 'ego' as the modern dictionary definition – 'a person's sense of self-esteem or self-importance'.

While ego isn't all bad, it can play a negative role in the way we manage our day-to-day relationships and communication. For example, in previous relationships during my twenties, I didn't do the best job of controlling my ego. The way in which this manifested for me was through how I processed certain types of advice and constructive criticism. When I was younger, I may have been approached with sound suggestions related to how I could be a better partner, but rather than process suggestions as something that may help me, my ego saw things as a personal attack: 'Why do they want me to change? Aren't I good enough? Why do they think badly of me?'. This in turn controlled the way I'd listen. Because I wouldn't. Instead of listening to understand, I would become highly defensive and closed off to constructive criticism of any kind. This behaviour significantly impacted my ability to take accountability. My ego was self-righteous and rarely interpreted my more negative behaviours as problematic. This further led to me becoming someone who pointed fingers. Instead of taking time out to reflect on my own issues, I would highlight something the other party did that was wrong. My ego was so sensitive to criticism of any kind that it refused to acknowledge that sometimes *I* was the problem. The only thing I was willing to process was how someone else may have contributed to the behaviour I was displaying.

For others, ego manifests through displays of competition. While competition can be healthy to some degree, in our romantic relationships it can often have a negative effect. When we allow our ego to see our lover as a competitor and not a supporter, we stop working together in partnership. We become obsessed with 'one-upping' them and focus less on what we gain from the relationship but more on what we bring to it versus what they bring. Alternatively, ego can create drama in some relationships. For certain people, ego multiplies solvable issues and revs them up. Ego may also see certain threats where there are none.

However ego manifests in relationships, one lesson I learned is that the negative elements of our ego really have no place in our connections with other people. We do our relationships a disservice when we allow our ego to control the way we navigate and the way we communicate with others.

If you ever find yourself having an ego-driven inter-action, things to ask yourself include:

- Is this person criticising me in a constructive way with the intention to help me become a better person?
- Do I disagree with what they are saying or am I just hurt that they don't view me as perfect?
- Is their feedback an accurate assessment of my behaviour?
- Will having this discussion improve the relationship for the both of us?
- Am I being combative because I don't like discussing my flaws?

Taking accountability isn't always easy, particularly when the discussion revolves around something you are doing badly or could do better. But accountability is important for self-growth and relationship growth. Accountability is also easier to take on when our ego is less sensitive to receiving feedback.

You are responsible for your own happiness

> *People may add to and subtract from your happiness, but they are not responsible for it. When we make the mistake of looking to our partner to fill a void, we give them power that they shouldn't have and responsibility that is unfair to them. The moment we assert that they are responsible for our happiness, we remove our own role as the captain of our life. We also blame them for our sorrow every time we find ourselves unhappy.*

This lesson isn't one that I learned solely through experience. I have to thank actor Will Smith for reinforcing this lesson in my life. It's a lesson he brought to the forefront of my mind after posting a video online in 2018 about his relationship with his wife Jada. In the video Will said: 'You cannot make a person happy. I thought that was a real deep idea. You can make a person smile. You can make a person feel good. You can make a person laugh. But, whether or not a person is happy is deeply, totally and utterly out of your control.'

This was something I had never really considered in great detail before. I was gripped by what Will shared and had to hear more. He went on to say: 'I remember the day I retired. I literally said to Jada that's it. I retire. I retire from trying to make you happy. I need you to go make yourself happy and just prove to me that it's even possible.'

Retiring from making your wife happy?! Surely that's a recipe for disaster I thought.

He concluded: 'We decided that we were going to find our individual internal private separate joy and then we're going to present ourselves to the relationship and to each other already happy. Not coming to each other begging with our empty cups out, demanding that she fill my cup. And demanding that she meet my needs. It's unfair and it's kind of unrealistic and can be destructive to place the responsibility for your happiness on anybody other than yourself.'

I've learned not to look up to other people's relationships (because you never know what goes on behind closed doors), but I do appreciate this aspect of the relationship Will Smith has with his wife. I appreciate the sentiment because as much as we may love people, our partners are not actually our 'other halves' and we are not incomplete without them. Seeing your partner as your 'other half' rids you of your wholeness and rids them of their individuality. They are not half of you and you are not half of them. You are both whole with or without each other. When you're in a relationship, you should celebrate your wholeness together.

Growing up – particularly as a heterosexual woman – I was led to believe that my life would become 'complete' with a man. As a young girl, I would watch movies about a damsel in distress who meets her Prince Charming, and suddenly all the issues she faced in life are resolved, and just like that, they live happily ever after. Even as I grew out of this harmful way of thinking, I still saw it being echoed around me. As someone who is highly visible on social media, my relationship status (or lack of) would often be brought to the forefront anytime an online troll wanted to diminish me in some way. Now, imagine how bad it gets as someone who writes about relationships? How dare I be single and write about love? How dare I be single in my thirties? I must be utterly miserable and incomplete because I don't have a man. Also, I must be a hideous person because nobody 'wants' me. Or at least, that's what the trolls would suggest.

Sadly, some people place so much emphasis on relationships that they can't actually fathom another person feeling complete without one. They can't fathom people making an active or deliberate choice not to settle and to be single until they find the right person for them. They can't fathom showing up to a relationship as a whole individual, which is actually quite unfortunate. Aspects of society have programmed people (mostly women) to be so relationship focused that we connect a great deal of our happiness to our partners, and I believe this does more harm than good.

Don't get me wrong, love is wonderful. I wouldn't be writing about it if it wasn't, but equally, having a romantic companion doesn't define us as people. Too many of us go through life believing that finding romantic love will complete us and suddenly our life will make sense – but this simply isn't the case. Love can undeniably contribute to an added layer of satisfaction in our life but it cannot satisfy the unsatisfied. True satisfaction with life relies on so much more. I have since learned with age, that it is my job to find happiness in my own life – whether or not a romantic partner is present. And when one is present, they most certainly have a role in helping to *preserve* my happiness but I don't expect them to create it – because they don't own it. I do.

Don't forget to celebrate your partner

> *It's very easy to complain about what we don't like in our partners and forget to celebrate what we do like. In relationships it's important to share compliments, provide words of affirmation and give praise where it's deserved. Don't speak up only when you are annoyed. Speak up when you are happy too.*

I want you to ask yourself a question. How many times have you complained or written a bad review when you received poor service or a poor product? Now ask yourself how many times you have shared feedback or written a positive review when you have received great service or a great product? Without knowing your answer, I'm going to assume that you have expressed dissatisfaction more than you have shared exceptional praise. I'm making this assumption because research suggests that the average person is almost three times more likely to leave a review after a negative experience, versus a positive one. I guess you could argue that it's human nature for people to focus more on the negative, and speak more regularly about being unhappy, than the opposite.

Complaints have a place in society and are usually very valid. However, our tendency to complain more than give praise can have a really damaging impact on our relationships.

Have you ever been in a relationship and felt like you were always being criticised? If so, how did that make you feel? Incapable? Useless? Underappreciated?

Admittedly, I've been on the opposite end of this example. I've been in a relationship where I was the complainer. This was largely down to feeling unhappy about certain elements of my relationship at the time, so my complaints had purpose, but the problem wasn't in my complaining, it was in my lack of praise. I was so frustrated by little negatives that I failed to appreciate big positives at times.

This lesson is simple, yet one that I believe truly helps relationships feel more positive.

Give praise when praise is due and appreciate people just as much as you want to be appreciated.

Section 3:
The Healing Stage

Heartbreak is an essential part of love. This is a bitter pill to swallow and I know you may be querying this sentence, but it's true. To love is to know loss, and this is relevant for 'forever' relationships as well as seasonal ones. Even when our romantic relationships are forever, our physical body is not, and in forever relationships we will 'lose people' when their body leaves this earth, or we will lose them when our body leaves it. Heartbreak is an essential part of loss. There is no escaping it.

No matter how sweet love is when we are in the midst of it, the sweetness rarely eradicates the bitterness we can feel at the end. Breakups can be incredibly tough to manage – particularly when they are out of our control.

In this section of my book I want to share lessons I learned about heartbreak, which may help you understand your own emotions if you are currently dealing with it. If you are not dealing with heartbreak at the moment, my lessons may help ease feelings from the past, or may even guide you in the future.

Don't reflect to the point that you dwell

Allow yourself time to feel and reflect, but don't reflect to the point that you dwell. It's unhealthy to deprive yourself of the opportunity to grieve after the breakdown of a relationship. Cry if you want to, and reflect if you want to, but also allow yourself the freedom to heal and move on.

The pain of a breakup can be devastating. It can encourage us to feel as if the world is coming to an end. Many people feel as if everything they have ever wanted and dreamed of has been taken away and they assume that they will never find joy or happiness again. I know this feeling. The flurry of emotions can trigger sadness, low mood or even depression. There's no knowing how you'll feel after you're no longer with the person you've loved the most, until it happens.

After a breakup, people often do one of three things. The first is pretend as if everything is okay, even when it isn't. When this happens to a person, they tend to feel very numb. The numbness deceives them into thinking they feel 'nothing' but that nothingness isn't nothingness at all. It's usually emotion so frighteningly overwhelming that their brain wants to stop them from processing it. Their brain flickers into defence mode and they feel empty, because admitting that they are not empty means processing what is taking place. 'They' is me. And 'I' am they.

After the breakup that changed my life (you know, the one that influenced me to start writing this book), I felt numb. Despite the relationship lasting numerous years, it was back to business within a day or two. I was so numb that I couldn't even bring myself to cry. I acted blasé and unbothered to the point I believed I actually was. 'Wow I'm so resilient,' I thought. But it seemed like everyone around me could see past that. In fact, I was so numb that it *concerned* the people around me. Surely, after six plus years in a relationship with someone, it's 'normal' to be distraught? Not me. In my mind I was perfectly fine. When the people closest to me would ask how I felt, my response would be 'it is what it is', or 'yeah I'm not going to waste my energy caring', or 'of course I'm fine, can't you see I'm fine?'.

When people feel numb, it's very easy to replace the vacant feeling with other not so helpful things. They may feel the need to self-medicate and as a result they may throw themselves into meaningless relationships, sex, alcohol, drugs or even their work. Anything which may distract them from confronting what is lying dormant inside. For me, it was work. At the time I was working a nine to five job and I threw myself into it as best as I could to distract myself from whatever it was I was denying. Until one day … I lost it. I had a complete meltdown in my office bathroom and that's when I realised I wasn't being strong and 'resilient'. I was just trying to convince myself that I was okay, which is what made me numb. But I wasn't okay.

The second thing people may do after a breakup, instead of feeling numb, is to feel so engrossed in emotion that it overpowers them to the point that they can do barely anything except focus on what they lost. This is what I've seen people close to me do. They sit in the emotion to the point that it swallows their whole being and controls the majority of their thoughts. They are unable to distract themselves even for a moment because all they can think about is the heartbreak. They cry for long periods and are on the verge of tears even after crying, fighting so hard to prevent themselves from crying some more. Nothing anyone can say can make them feel better. Instead, they wallow in the emotion for an extended period of time. Maybe this is what you do?

The third thing people do is strike a balance, which I think is the healthiest way to begin healing. Unlike myself, who would bury emotions and present a seemingly unbothered façade to the world, people in the third category allow themselves to feel. They permit themselves to cry and they embrace all the emotions running through them. They immerse themselves in the sadness momentarily. They are not scared of confronting the reality that they are hurt and they understand that expression of this hurt is healthy. However, unlike people who wallow and allow themselves to be totally consumed for long periods of time, they feel what they need to feel without dwelling. They understand that relationships come and go, and while losses are painful, they do not define us as people and they should not control our lives.

Giving yourself permission to grieve is an important part of heartbreak, but another very important part is giving yourself permission to move on.

Sometimes you miss the routine

> *Sometimes what we miss after a breakup is the familiarity. The presence of another human being. Talking to someone day and night. Waking up next to someone. Sleeping with someone. Going out and having fun with someone. But it's not the character of the person we miss. It's the routine we had with them.*

Most people who have gone through a breakup have experienced that feeling of longing not so soon afterwards. Sometimes it's for the person they lost, other times that feeling tricks them into believing they miss the person they lost, even when they don't.

To help you determine whether you actually miss a person, ask yourself how they made you feel when you were with them. Ask yourself if they contributed to your wellbeing in a positive way. Ask yourself if you flourished in their presence. Ask yourself if being around them brought out the best in you. If you answer 'no' to these questions, it's safe to say you miss the routine that comes with having a companion in your life. You don't miss *the* person, you miss having *a* person. And that's completely okay.

Missing the routine that comes with having a partner isn't something you should ever feel ashamed of. After all, one of the things which makes us human is a longing for companionship. Most of us want to feel like we're experiencing the world alongside someone, which is why the routine that comes with a relationship can feel satisfying, even when the relationship fundamentally is not. With this said, it's very important for us to recognise when this longing is attached to a routine and not a person. The inability to recognise the difference can often prompt people to cling on to partners that aren't good for them, under the false belief that without them they don't feel whole. An inability to recognise when you miss the routine can have you believing that your feeling of longing can only be remedied by the person you were previously with. When in fact, you're comfortable with the familiarity and what you desire is the routine, which can be fulfilled by anybody.

To further determine whether you miss the person or whether you miss the routine, ask yourself when your feelings emerge. Are they constant or do you find your-self missing the person at key points that highlight the fact you are now single? For example, do you miss them at parties? When you go to bed at night? At family func-tions? When you're alone with your thoughts and nobody else is around? This could be an indicator that your feelings are connected to the routine instead of the person.

If you're still not sure whether it is indeed the routine that you miss, write down what you miss about the person that can't be easily fulfilled by anyone else. If you find yourself struggling to write things, then that's another good indicator that you miss the routine.

Sometimes relationships are worse than we realise

> We don't always know how bad a relationship is when we're in the eye of the storm.
> Sometimes it takes hindsight to really highlight what we went through.

Have you ever reflected on how certain people have treated you in the past and thought, 'wow, they were way worse than I understood at the time'? I know I have.

I've been in a relationship which involved me dismissing negative behaviours. Even when I saw the worst of them, I was sure they meant well and had a good heart. I was blind to their character flaws and indiscretions because I let attraction get the better of me. Even after I walked away from the relationship, I still had a soft spot for them. It was as if I had forgotten about all the terrible things they put me through, until one day, I really took the time out to sit and reflect. I replayed all the lies, all the distrust, all the abusive behaviour and I was actually shocked to realise that I had gone through all that with them. The foulness of their behaviour didn't actually completely hit me until I wrote a list. I looked at the list and felt numb. 'Toni, you really went through all THAT?'

Sometimes we don't actually understand how bad a relationship is until we are no longer in the relationship. It can often take distance and hindsight for us to fully assess. This assessment usually takes some time. There's a short window after a breakup where people feel immediately hurt and lonely, and often want to reconcile with their ex-partner. They're susceptible to forgiving things they shouldn't forgive or accepting things they shouldn't accept, but I think it's important to ride this time out because once this period ceases, that's when the rose-tinted glasses come off. That's when we reflect on the relationship with a better understanding of what truly occurred, because we are not riddled with feelings of loneliness. We've become more accustomed to being on our own, so our assessment of our ex-partner is clearer. Time and experience is sometimes required to fully understand the trauma some people put you through.

One thing I recommend post breakup is to write experiences down. Make a list of good experiences and bad experiences and read them out loud. This is one thing that helped me to truly understand the quality of my relationships based on what they really were and not what I wanted them to be.

When you're writing all these things down, it's also important for you be compassionate with yourself in the process. I say this because you may find yourself writing lots of good things down and subsequently beat yourself up for 'losing' your partner. Alternatively you may write lots of bad things down and end up criticising yourself for 'letting them happen'. When it comes to the latter, I've learned not to reinforce the notion that 'people do what we allow' because it puts the onus and responsibility in the hands of the victim. People always do what they want to do and what they are capable of. Perhaps you experienced more than you may have if you had left earlier, but during traumatic events and times of crisis, it's not always as simple. Especially when you don't know any better. For example, when I went through my own experience, I didn't fully understand the range of abusive behaviour people can exhibit. I didn't really understand green and red flags and how to look out for them. I did what I knew at the time.

Similarly, if you end up feeling bad because you've reflected on a previous relationship and realised that your partner was much nicer than you gave them credit for, and you didn't really appreciate them, then it's important that you see it as a lesson to help you in the future. Allow it to reinforce the fact we must let people know how valuable they are to us when we have them and we must rely not just on our words to express our love, but also our actions.

Beware of exes who want to stroke their ego

> *Sometimes people re-enter your life not because they genuinely miss you and want to add value, but because you don't miss them, and their ego wants confirmation that they still have access to you.*

Once upon a time in my life, I used to regard the return of an ex as a good thing – something that signifies my value and appeal. Surely if they're contacting me again, it means they miss me? Surely nobody would miss someone who wasn't worth missing? Surely if they want another chance, they're going to be better and they want to add value? Sadly I quickly learned that this simply isn't the case all of the time. Unfortunately some people use others as an ego boost. They have no intention of contributing to the other person's life in a positive way but they acknowledge the positive role the other person has played in their own life. So when they are in need of affection, words of affirmation, support, intimacy or companionship they return. They return and they remain until they have taken what they needed to take, and then they leave again to fulfil whatever desire they wanted to fulfil when they left in the first place.

Alternatively, there are people who may return because they despise the thought of anyone else being with you, despite the fact they don't want to be with you. For whatever narcissistic reason, they view you as something they own and they reappear in your life as a form of emotional manipulation. They understand that communicating with you has the potential to reignite feelings, which in turn makes it harder for you to move on.

So, how do you spot these people? Well people with these awful intentions do a great reappearing and disappearing act. They have a tendency of showing up out of nowhere and ghosting out of nowhere too. They also rarely have explanations for their 'disappearance', because coming clean would highlight that you are an option to them, not a priority. They have you questioning where you stand with them and they never make a firm decision regarding the outcome they would like from your correspondence. The communication is rarely about 'getting back together' and instead, they focus on getting something – whether it's sex, your attention, your time or even gifts. Their priority is to use you or interrupt your healing.

If you notice these behaviours in an ex, do what you need to do to implement boundaries.

Implement boundaries during a breakup

> *Implementing boundaries during a breakup is just as important as implementing boundaries during a relationship. Have you recently broken up with someone? Moving on from them will require the implementation of some boundaries on your part. Assert who won't have access to you anymore. Assert what you will and won't expose yourself to. Assert what you will and won't accept.*

Many people who have experienced a breakup know that it doesn't always come with a 'clean break' from the other person. After all, if you have been in a relationship with someone for some time, it can be difficult to let that person go. One of the best ways to ensure that you allow yourself the opportunity to move on is through actioning certain boundaries which will help you limit access to your ex.

Limiting access to exes is an important part of moving on because maintaining access often results in one or both parties maintaining a hold over the other – whether that be physically, emotionally or mentally. This hold can often get in the way of mentally growing out of the relationship, emotionally bonding with other people and even physically making the effort to live a different type of day-to-day routine.

One boundary which you may want to consider includes unfollowing (or blocking) an ex-partner on social media. Some people may consider this to be a fairly drastic move but for many people, social media plays a significant role in their daily life. If you are hoping to move on from someone, it would be unwise to allow yourself the opportunity to check up on their online life each day. Now that's not to say you have to unfollow them forever, but in the initial stage of trying to get over that person, it's helpful to you if you limit your online access to them.

Physical access is just as important to limit. Plenty of people believe they possess the capacity to separate their physical desires from their emotions, when frankly, they don't. Separating emotions from sex isn't always easy in general – let alone when you've shared a romantic past with someone. At times, even when a person believes feeding their physical desire isn't impacting their ability to move on, it is. It's normal for people to have intimate needs but fulfilling those needs at the expense of limiting your ability to move past an old relationship, isn't worth it.

Another boundary to consider is general communication. Those 'hey stranger' texts might seem like a good idea in moments of loneliness, but the repercussions can be significant. Before messaging or calling ex-partners, consider what you're trying to get out of the interaction. Why do you want to talk to them? The conversation people hope to generate when they do this is usually a part-time fix for a deeper reason. Getting to the root of the reason is more important.

Healing from a breakup is like kicking a bad habit. It's easier to tackle when you limit your access. It's easier to move forward when you set boundaries.

Not all losses are losses

> *Sometimes we have to lose certain people to find ourselves. Sometimes what we lost is what was holding us back. Sometimes what feels like a loss in the moment is a win for the long term.*

As I'm writing about this lesson, I'm taken back down memory lane – to a memory from a few years ago. This memory involved the breakdown of my longest relationship. The relationship took up most of my twenties and played a massive role in who I am today. I love who I am, and I am grateful to that relationship for shaping me in the way it did.

When it broke down, I was hurt, but being the relatively pragmatic person that I am, I knew it wasn't worth dwelling on for too long, and instead I took steps to heal and grow. One of the key steps I took was to gather my thoughts and redefine who I am. For most of my adulthood I had been attached to this person, and my adult identity felt very connected to them – so I went on a quest to figure out more about me. I began investing in things I enjoyed, I began taking on new hobbies and I started journaling my feelings and replaying what I did right and what I could change in the future. I did all of this with self-compassion.

Eventually, this led to me feeling more comfortable in my own skin and more comfortable with speaking my mind (something that I didn't do enough of in the relationship). I summoned the courage to share some of my learnings online and before I knew it, I had amassed a large online following (of mostly women), who could really relate to my own thoughts, experiences, observations and emotions. My online platform then grew from strength to strength. Before I knew it, I had quit my nine to five job to start my own company and focus on my creativity. Then not long after that, I signed a very impressive book deal as a first time author to develop this book you're currently reading. I then went on to win a BBC commission for my very own podcast. My life changed in a matter of two years, and these changes may have been unattainable if not for the 'loss' I experienced, which inevitably became a win. Looking back at how my life progressed after that breakup, I wouldn't change a thing and, arguably, it was one of the best things that could have happened to me.

I'm very aware that not every breakup story mirrors mine and not everyone will experience a life-changing career shift in the same way I did. My story is uncommon and for a lot of people, the first year after a breakup is one of the most difficult years of their life. Some people grapple with a constant state of low mood and feel utterly destroyed. The sheer thought of getting out of bed in the morning is overwhelming for them, let alone thinking about ways they can channel their emotions productively.

But with this said, even through our darkest moments, we have the opportunity to make life-changing shifts and life-changing choices. When we experience heartbreak, we are often presented with a crossroads, and we are forced to make certain decisions about our future. These decisions tend to centre our priorities. What do I do now? What will I stop doing? Where do I want to be located? All of these decisions can be seen as risks but as I've mentioned previously in this book, the biggest rewards usually come with an element of risk and being forced into making certain decisions that you may have previously dismissed, can be life-changing.

I don't expect people to heal like Wolverine after a relationship ends. Healing is a journey, which takes time. But what I don't want you to do is assume that you have lost a part of yourself or that you are less important in some way, simply because someone has broken up with you. You lost a companion, but you are very much a whole person with bright possibilities and a promising future, as long as you give yourself the permission to believe this. You are the author of your own life and the writer of your own story. Do not think your story has to stop because your relationship has ended. Instead, realise that a new chapter has simply begun. You have lost a relationship, but you have gained more freedom. More freedom to focus solely on yourself and consider what you want this next chapter of your life to look like. Every day, when you are struggling to get out of bed, ask yourself how you want to write this chapter, and remind yourself that you are in control of your outcomes. You might be grieving a loss now, but in losing one thing, you can find another. You can find yourself.

Invested time is only a waste if you see it like that

> *It's very easy to walk away from a relationship and think about the time you 'wasted' or the things you 'lost', but sometimes healing can be facilitated by a change in perspective. What did you gain in that time? A better sense of self? A clearer vision of what you want? What did you learn that will help you in life, and in your next relationship?*

As I am writing this book, I've spent over ten years of my life in relationships. Ten years of being connected to people who are no longer in my life. My longest relationship ended when I was in my late twenties – your 'prime years' as people like to say. This is a damaging societal concept to be perfectly honest. It's a concept which led to me beating myself up for remaining in that relationship for six years of my life. It led to me feeling resentful and holding my ex accountable for a decision we made jointly. It contributed to me panicking about the future and worrying about whether I'd find love again or 'in time'. To regain my peace, I had to do multiple things. The first was throw away the concept of being in my 'prime' in my twenties.

When I took a step back to examine and speak to some of the women I really admired, many of them have felt happier, more attractive, more successful and more confident with age. I came to the realisation that if I kept saying my prime was in my twenties then I'd encourage myself to plateau. I didn't want this to be a self-fulfilling prophecy, so I told myself that my prime is whenever I want it to be. Fast forward to my thirties and I'm happy to say they've been the best years of my life to date. I'm not sure if this would have been true if I didn't let go of the mindset that was previously holding me back.

Once I got over the fact that I wasn't going to allow my twenties to be the best years of my life, I immediately felt less resentful, less regretful and less angry. My peace strengthened even more when I began to ask myself what I learned from the relationship that would help me become a better person overall. Despite the fact my ex and I had our differences at times, he had many good traits, and our relationship *did* teach me a range of valuable lessons. I left the relationship being less judgemental, being more open to people's differences, being ambitious, being more aware of the need to prioritise myself in my life, being more willing to take risks and much more. On one hand, I could have continued to see the time I spent with him as a waste, but on the other hand, I decided that wouldn't help me. Instead I saw our time together as a season of my life that was destined. A season that contributed to me becoming a well-rounded person, as a result of learning a series of lessons throughout that relationship. In fact, I took my learning so literally that I made a book about it. Who would have thought?

A part of me did ask myself whether my perspective would have been so optimistic if I had experienced a very turbulent relationship with him. The thing is, I *have* had a turbulent relationship in the past with someone else. Prior to my longest relationship, I had been in a relationship that made me feel small. It felt like a total and utter waste of time. I left that relationship feeling like a broken version of my original self, but through healing I discovered that the negativity I had been through didn't have to define my outlook. Instead, I took that negative experience and used it to shape what I wanted in the future. It also formed the foundation for what I would and would not tolerate moving forward.

I want you to know that relationships (whether long-lasting and positive, or not), provide us with a world of experience and lessons that we can take on to future relationships. Past bonds shape the way we date and often help us to really understand what we want and what we don't want in a partner. Relationships also give us insight into our own behaviours. For some people, past relationships have highlighted aspects of their character that they want to change or aspects of their character that they may love. In addition, some people are lucky enough to have ex-partners who helped shape them in positive ways. The experiences and lessons they have taken away have actually made them better partners for lovers in the future – whether they know this or not. Even when people have had terrible ex-partners, their experiences and lessons have the capacity to improve the way they navigate relationships in future for themselves.

Are there some relationships we may have spent more time in than we should have? Most definitely. But never see any additional time as a *waste of time* and don't beat yourself up for things you now know in hindsight. An unwillingness to depart a failing relationship doesn't make you weak or dumb. Sometimes we still have growth we need to undertake, lessons we need to learn or plans we need to put in place before we completely depart. Also, most relationships are seasonal and won't last forever. But just because they're not 'forever relationships' doesn't mean we gained absolutely nothing from them.

Never compromise your character to teach somebody a lesson

> *After heartbreak, too many of us compromise our character in an attempt to teach the other person some kind of lesson. However, when we step out of our nature to do things we wouldn't ordinarily do, we may feel vindicated in the moment but after that we will have to live with the impact of our actions. Before you react in anger, ask yourself if the best version of yourself would be happy with what you are about to do.*

Heartbreak can be devastating. Particularly when someone has broken your trust in the process. Being cheated on is one form of heartbreak that can sometimes encourage us to harbour feelings of intense anger. This anger can very quickly turn into thoughts of vengeance, particularly if our ego is front and centre during this time. When this happens, at the forefront of a person's mind isn't how they can peacefully heal. At the forefront of their mind is utter shock that someone they love could hurt them in this way. At the forefront of their mind is an anger so strong that it feeds a thirst for vengeance. If you've ever felt this feeling before, then you know exactly what I'm talking about. You want them to feel how you feel. You want them to experience the impact of what they did. You want them to know the pain you're faced with.

Unprocessed anger and a thirst for vengeance can lead people to compromise their character in a range of ways. Perhaps they think the only way to heal is to cheat back. Perhaps they believe the pain can be shared through destruction of the other person's personal property. Perhaps they want to damage the other person's career or their reputation with other people. Whatever they desire, these negative responses to experiencing pain can have a more significant impact on the person looking for vengeance.

When we take actions that go against the values and principles we hold for ourselves, we are compromising our character. We are asserting that our experience of pain justifies doing things we would typically never do. Might we hurt the person in the process? Yes. But we also have to live with the fact that we have done something we can never take back.

Sometimes these things also have significant negative repercussions for us. I've heard stories of people who participated in revenge porn, property destruction or worse – at the end of the day, justice was served and they suffered more due to their actions. I've heard stories of people revenge cheating only for them to feel like they gave themselves away to someone who was undeserving, simply to cause pain to another person. It even seems silly when writing it out.

As someone who has been deeply hurt by a partner in the past, I understand why someone may want to initiate revenge but this is where emotional intelligence and self-love comes in. You need to make the effort to regulate your emotions – no matter how intense or negative they are. You also need to recognise your worth and value because when you do, you realise the greatest form of 'revenge' is walking away because they will lose their access to you.

If you make the decision to stay after someone's indiscretions (this choice is yours and yours alone), revengeful behaviour on your part will negatively impact your ability to move on from the past. It could also encourage your partner to feel justified in their previous actions. This is why if you don't walk away, you should hold the person accountable without doing anything compromising on your part. If they are remorseful and administer changed behaviour, focus on moving forward and healing, not revenge.

Missing someone who wasn't good for you doesn't make you weak

> *In fact, to miss someone and still assert that you are better off without them is powerful. There's so much power in allowing yourself to feel and process your emotions without your emotions completely controlling you. The self-awareness coupled with the self-regulation is a sign of emotional intelligence. You manage your emotions. They don't manage you.*

Immediately after the breakdown of my longest relationship, I struggled with a range of emotions initially. One of them included feeling torn about the fact I still missed the other person, despite knowing I was better off without them at the time. There was a lot about our relationship that worked well, but there was also a lot about our relationship that screamed 'this isn't going to work' and deep down I knew the breakup was for the best. Despite this, I still experienced a sadness and longing that confused me. I was the happiest I had ever been upon leaving the relationship, but their departure still hurt me.

One difficult thing about breakups is the imprint people leave on you. You cannot erase the time you spent with them – not the memories, not the intimacy, nothing. All you can do is try your very best to accept that what is in the past, will remain there.

After my personal experience, it became very clear to me that accepting the fact someone may not have been good for you, doesn't mean you automatically stop missing them. Despite some bad times, you may miss the good times you experienced. You may miss the way they made you feel during those good times. You may miss the laughs you shared with one another, or the way they smiled, or the way they looked at you. You may even miss the routine (you should know what I mean).

Whatever you miss, I want you to know that you can heal and still miss people sometimes. You can heal and still experience fleeting thoughts regarding what once was. Why is that you ask? Healing involves acceptance and forgiveness, as well as a willingness to move forward. You can do all these things and still reflect on the past.

All of this leads to the further realisation that healing isn't linear. When we see healing as linear, we do ourselves no favours. We do not allow ourselves the grace or compassion to hurt sometimes, to cry sometimes, to miss people sometimes. When we see healing as linear, we beat ourselves up when we respond to our healing journey in a very human way.

Throughout my section on the healing stage, I've shared lessons about learning from your relationship, about writing your own story, about creating boundaries, about shifting your perspective … But I also don't want to pretend that healing will be easy. You will have your good days when you are healing, and you will have your bad days. Healing is many things, but it's not simple, it's not a race, and it's not linear. It's difficult, it's a journey and it comes with ups and downs.

'But what if I've tried to heal and I still have love for them?' – it's okay to love people from afar.

I have dated people that I still have love for to this day. Am I *in love* with them in a way that sparks intimate desires? No. But do I love them to the point that I want them to be happy? Yes. Do I love them to the point that I want them to find love? Yes. Do I love them to the point that I want them to prosper in life? Yes. Do I love them to the point that I clap for their achievements? Yes. I want to see them happy, healthy, successful, in love, joyous and pleased with their life. But I also want to have love for·them from a distance – for my own serenity.

I learned the value of loving people from a distance when loving them close up impacted my inner peace. In an ideal world, we'd all be 'friends' with our exes after a breakup, but the world isn't ideal, and too often, maintaining communication with certain people can sometimes cause more harm than good (hence the value of boundaries). For example, if you've been through a breakup that hindered your self-esteem, toyed with your stress levels and impacted your health, it's unlikely that the aftermath of these incidences will simply 'disappear' once you decide to remain friends. It's very hard to heal from certain types of relationship trauma when you have a direct line to the person who caused that trauma in the first place. Alternatively, if you were in a relationship that was great in many ways, it's still hard to move on when you're constantly reminded of what was.

Loving from afar is healthier than loving from up close when relationships end, and missing people when they end is normal.

Conclusion

You're at the end of my book now, and I can only hope that everything I wish I knew earlier are things you know now. I hope I was able to provide some of the big sisterly advice I missed out on. I have made a few mistakes in relationships but I've done a lot of good too, and what I am most proud of to date is being able to grow and share my learnings with you.

When it comes to matters of the heart, we won't always get it right – no matter how experienced we are. One thing I know for certain though, is that our experiences help us to grow and there is always something to learn. Dating can be a bit of a jungle at times, loving isn't easy and healing is hard – but all stages are important when developing romantic relationships.

The conversation and learning doesn't have to end here though. Let's continue to learn together: #*IWIKTE*.

Toni Tone

x